LORD
BYRON'S
RELISH

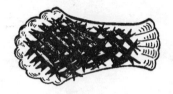

LORD BYRON'S RELISH
is a collection of recipes for Regency dishes gathered from cookery books of the period: books which Lord Byron, (as voracious in his eating habits as in his love life) is known to have consulted. To these the editor, Wilma Paterson, has added relevant extracts from Byron's poems and letters, the writings of his friends; also her own notes, with a postscript on Byron's eating habits which suggests that, like many part-time gluttons, he was anorexic. The book culminates in a menu and recipes for the mouth-watering banquet at the end of Byron's greatest poem, the comic epic DON JUAN.

Wilma Paterson is a Scottish composer whose chamber music has been commissioned and performed at international festivals in Britain and overseas. She has also had her own culinary advice programme on BBC Scotland, and is the author of—
A COUNTRY CUP
SHOESTRING GOURMET
A FOUNTAIN OF GARDENS

LORD BYRON'S RELISH

The fundamental principal of all
Is what ingenious cooks the relish call;
For when the markets end in loads of food,
They all are tasteless till that makes them good.
FROM DR. KING'S *HINTS FOR THE TABLE*

Regency Recipes
with notes
Culinary & Byronic
by
Wilma Paterson

DOG & BONE
GLASGOW 1990

THIS BOOK WAS
FIRST PUBLISHED
IN SCOTLAND 1990
BY
DOG & BONE
175 QUEEN VICTORIA
DRIVE, GLASGOW

DESIGNED BY
ALASDAIR GRAY
TYPESET BY
DONALD SAUNDERS
PRINTED, BOUND
BY
COX & WYMAN,
CARDIFF ROAD, READING

ISBN 1 872536 02 6

TO
A.J.G.

The waste at ball-suppers was almost incredible. Ude states that he has known balls, where, the next day, in spite of the pillage of a pack of foot-men, he has seen twenty or thirty hams, 150 or 200 carved fowls, and forty or fifty tongues, given away; jellies melted on the tables; pastry, pâtés, pies, and lobster salads, all heaped up in the kitchen, and strewed about the passages, completely dis-figured by the manner in which it was necessary to take them from the dishes in which they were served.

TABLE OF

SOUPS

SAUCES

CONTENTS

SHELLFISH

FISH

POULTRY AND GAME

TABLE OF

MEAT

CONTENTS

VINEGARS AND KETCHUPS

TABLE OF

CONTENTS

VARIOUS RECEIPTS

THE DINNER FROM *DON JUAN*

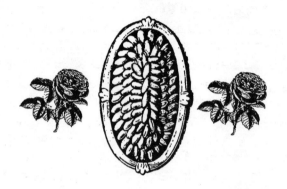

THE EDITOR'S PREFACE

I have lived in far countries, abroad, or in the agitating world at home ... so that almost all I have written has been mere – passion, it is true, of different kinds, but always passion ...

AND NEARLY TWO HUNDRED YEARS after the poet's death this extraordinary man continues to arouse controversy and to excite strong passions and unprecedented devotions. New books and papers are published every year on aspects of his life and work, his marriage, his loves, his travels and his personal charms. I make no apology for adding to the list. This little book is a comprehensive and practical cookery book compiled from contemporary sources with which the poet was familiar, and as well as giving some insight, I hope, into Byron's character gives also a glimpse of manners and social conventions at a time when English cookery was enjoying a golden age.

Byron's poetry was not taught in my school, and when I did first read him – not so many years ago – I was bowled over – by his wit and exuberance, by the breadth of his understanding, by his fun, mischief and acidity, but above all by his immensely loveable nature and charisma. I was struck too by the unusual gastric preoccupation which runs through the poetry, prose, letters and journals – a preoccupation approaching the obsessional.

Lord Byron's Relish is made up of references to food, cookery and eating in his poetry, letters and journals, and to reference by his family and friends to his eating habits, likes and dislikes and to his many ecccentricities.

The image of the dissipated English Lord dies hard,

and while this was certainly one aspect of an immensely complicated character, even a cursory glance at his writings will tell you that there is another story – painfully sad, indeed tragic, which I have touched upon in my postscript.

The recipes have been taken unaltered from popular cookery books of the period, with which Byron was familiar, and they are remarkably clear and simple, and present the modern cook with few problems. Hannah Glasse's *The Art of Cookery, Made Plain and Easy* which was first published in 1747 and ran into many editions over the next hundred years is a practical, no-nonsense book intended for the use of servants rather than for Chefs in great houses. Little is known about Mrs Glasse but she is thought to have been the wife of a London lawyer, and she wrote two other books besides the *Cookery* – *The Compleat Confectioner* and *The Servant's Directory.* Dr. Johnson said he could have written better himself ('Women cannot write a good book about cookery') but none the less it appears to have been the one used in his household.

Mrs Rundell's *A New System of Domestic Cookery* was published by Byron's publisher John Murray in 1807 and rivalled Mrs Glasse's for popularity with seventy editions and many plagiarised versions. A personal friend of the Publisher's, she wrote her book for the instruction of her daughter without any thought of financial gain. It became one of Murray's most valuable properties however, and he and Mrs Rundell eventually fell out over his handling of it and resorted to the law courts in order to settle their differences.

Mrs Raffald was trained in the kitchen of a Cheshire

country house, where she married the gardener and had sixteen daughters in eighteen years, during which time she also kept a confectionery shop in Manchester and ran three Lancashire inns, besides writing her book – *The Experienced English House-Keeper, For the Use and Ease of Ladies, House-Keepers, Cooks, etc.*

William Kitchiner was the son of a coal-porter who made a fortune in Bow Street as a coal-merchant and so could send his son to Eton and University. His medical degree however was from Glasgow so he couldn't practise in London, but his father had left him a great deal of money and William devoted himself to science and the entertainment of his friends. *The Cook's Oracle,* which was first published in 1817, is delightful and full of interest. Kitchiner admired French cookery but was irritated by 'those high-bred English epicures who cannot eat anything dressed by an English cook, and cannot endure the sight of the best bill of fare unless it is written in pretty good bad French.'

Eustache Ude was an emigré who worked in Britain after the Revolution as Chef to first the Earl of Sefton then to the Duke of York, and when he introduced the light sandwich supper during the Regency, he was accused of starving the nation to death by his rivals. Byron took the dishes for the dinner in Canto XV of *Don Juan* from Ude's *The French Cook, a system of fashionable, practical and economical Cookery, adapted to the use of English families.*

About the language of the recipes: since the words and spelling are part of the period's flavour these have not been modernised or made consistent. For example, what the

British now call *ketchup* and the Americans *catsup* appears in both forms, and sometimes with the variant *catchup*: but all three are kinds of piquant sauce containing vinegar, and therefor listed separately from the other sauces. This short glossary may be helpful.

Page 37 – *sippets:* small pieces of toast or fried bread

    50 – *drawing*: disembowelling

           helping: serving

           trail: entrail

    65 – *morel*: edible spring fungus

    69 – *pluck*: heart, lungs and liver

    76 – *soy*: soya sauce

    85 – *spattle*: spatula, beater

           powder blue: an edible dye used to aid whitening

    96 – *merellas*: morello cherries (small, dark, sour)

102 – *storax*: a vanilla-like scent

           gum benjamin: dried, scented resin

           cypress-powder: powdered cypress root

Ude's English is shown at its most peculiarly Gallic in the recipes for the menu Byron gave in Canto XV of *Don Juan*. A separate glossary is given before this on page 112.

TABLE OF DATES

1788 George Gordon Byron, the poet, born 22 January with a deformed foot.

1789 Taken to Aberdeen by his mother.

1791 Death of his father, Captain Byron.

1792 Attends day school in Aberdeen. Childhood happy in spite of money problems and his mother's alternating tantrums and effusions. Becomes heir to the title.

1796 Idealised devotion to eight-year-old Mary Duff.

1797 Calvinistic May Gray, his nurse, begins his sexual experience.

1798 Death of his great-uncle, Lord William Byron, 'the wicked Lord'. Byron inherits his title and Newstead Abbey, heavily encumbered by debts. Mrs Byron, her son and May Gray move to Newstead.

1799 Excruciating and ineffective treatment for his club foot.

1800 Passion for his cousin Margaret Parker inspires his first attempts at poetry.

1801 At Harrow until 1805. Falls in love with Mary Chaworth.

1805 Mary Chaworth rejects him and marries John Musters. Augusta (his half-sister) comes to Harrow for Speech Day. Byron enters Trinity College, Cambridge.

1809   Attains majority and takes seat in House of Lords. Journeys to Lisbon, Seville, Cadiz, Gibraltar, Malta, Albania, Missolonghi, Athens.

1810   Leaves Athens for Smyrna. Constantinople, then returns to Athens for ten months.

1811   Sails for England. Death of Mrs Byron, drowning of friend Matthews. Depressed by the loss of other young friends. Corresponds with Augusta.

1812   Speeches in the House of Lords. Affairs with Caroline Lamb and others. Meets Annabella Milbanke, proposes and is refused.

1813   Byron much in London Society. Afair with Augusta. Confides in Lady Melbourne.

1814   Byron's daughter, Madora Leigh, born to Augusta. Engaged to Annabella Milbanke.

1815   Married at Seaham. Settled in London. Meets Sir Walter Scott. Daughter, Augusta Ada, born. Lady Byron alienated.

1816   Lady Byron leaves London for her father's house. Deed of separation drawn up. Byron snubbed by London society. Acute financial difficulties. Claire Clairmont begins liaison with him. Prepares to leave for the Continent. Public auction of his library. With his servant Fletcher and Dr Polidori, Byron leaves England for ever. Travels through Belgium. Waterloo, the Rhine. Rents Villa Diodati on Lake

Geneva, Shelley, Mary Godwin and Claire Clairmont living nearby. Tour of Lake Geneva with Shelley, travels in the Alps with Hobhouse. Milan and Venice. Affair with Marianna Segati. Many casual affairs with lower-class women.

1817 Claire Clairmont gives birth to Allegra, Byron's daughter. Byron has fever after the Carnival season. Sets out for Rome, visiting Padua, Ferrara, Bologna, Florence. Venice and turbulent affair with Margarita Cogni begins. Hears that Newstead Abbey has been sold, gives instructions for paying of debts.

1818 Carnival festivity. Gonorreah. Continued dissipations. Allegra is brought to Venice. He moves to Palazzo Mocenigo. Shelley visits.

1819 Another illness. Begins liaison with Countess Guiccioli. Teresa's husband and her father Count Gamba try to separate the lovers.

1820 Byron lives at Palazzo Guiccioli in Ravenna with Teresa and her husband. Pope grants appeal for separation. Byron becomes friendly with Pietro Gamba, Teresa's brother, and joins a revolutionary society.

1821 Places Allegra in Convent of Bagnacavallo. Moves to Casa Lanfranchi in Pisa, contented in Pisa circle for a while (Shelleys, Edward and Jane Williams, Medwin, Taffe and the Gambas).

TABLE OF DATES

1822 Byron and Teresa sit for the sculptor Bartolini.
Inheritance after the death of his mother-in-law
doubles his income. Death of Allegra. Moves to
Villa Dupuy, Montenero near Leghorn. Shelley and
Williams drowned. Cremation of their remains.
Byron becomes ill during a swim. Health poor.

1823 Begins a brief association with Lord and Lady
Blessington and Count Alfred D'Orsay. Rekindled
interest in Greek war for independence. Has Pietro
Gamba tell Teresa of his plan to go to Greece.

1824 Plans an assault against Lepanto. Has severe con-
vulsions. Frequently depressed as military and
political circumstances worsen. Health deteriorates.
He no longer expects to achieve Greek unity. Final
illness begins and is aggravated by bungling of
doctors. Byron dies (19 April), his body is taken to
England and buried in the Hucknall Torkard Church
in Nottinghamshire.

SOUPS

They made a most superior mess of broth;
A thing which poesy but seldom mentions,
But the best dish that e' er was cooked
                              since Homer's
Achilles order'd dinner for new comers.
                    DON JUAN, CANTO II, cxxiii

Soups and broths held an important place in the Georgian kitchen and were also the basis of many of the elaborate sauces for the entrées of a grand dinner. They were very extravagent by today's standards and often required enormous quantities of beef, veal, ham and poultry. Certainly they were very nourishing. Augusta was always pleased to see her brother partaking of a homely broth – and particularly when she felt his health was poorly, or his stomach weak.

SCOTCH BARLEY-BROTH, with Boiled Mutton, or *Bouilli Ordinaire*.

To from three to six pounds of beef or mutton, according to the quantity of broth wanted, put cold water in the proportion of a quart to a pound, – a quarter-pound of Scotch barley, or more or less as may suit the meat and the water, and a spoonful of salt unless the meat is already slightly salted. To this put a large cupful of white pease, or split grey pease, unless in the season when old green pease are to be had cheap, a double quantity of which must be put in with the other vegetables, using less barley. Skim very carefully as long as any scum rises, then draw aside the pot, and let the broth boil slowly for an hour, at which time put to it two young carrots and turnips cut in dice, and two or three onions sliced. A quarter of an hour before the broth is ready, add a little parsley picked and chopped, – or the white part of three leeks may be used instead of onions, and a head of celery sliced instead of the parsley seasoning; but celery requires longer boiling

Scotch broth is homely and nourishing and was almost certainly staple fare for Byron while a child in Aberdeen.

Stockpot & Ladle.

THE OLD SCOTCH WHITE SOUP,
or *Soupe à la Reine*

Take a large knuckle of the whitest veal, well broken and soaked, a white fowl skinned, or two chickens, a quarter pound of well-coloured lean, undressed bacon, lemon-thyme, onions, carrot, celery, and a white turnip, a few white peppercorns, and two blades of mace. Boil for about two hours; skim repeatedly and carefully during that time. When the stock is well tasted, strain it off. It will form a jelly. When to be used, take off the surface-fat, clear off the sediment, and put the jelly into a tin sauce-pan, or a stew-pan freshly tinned; boil for a half hour, and serve on a couple of rounds of a small French roll; or with macaroni, previously soaked, and stewed in the soup till perfectly soft; or vermicelli. This is plain white soup. It is raised to LORRAINE soup as follows: Take a half pound of sweet almonds blanched (that is scalded and the husks rubbed off), the hard-boiled yolks of three eggs, and the skinned breast and white parts of a cold roast fowl; beat the almonds to a paste in a mortar, with a little water to prevent their oiling; mince very finely the fowl and eggs, and some breadcrumbs.Add to this hash an English pint or more of the stock, lemon-peel, and a scrape of nutmeg; bring it to boil, and put to it a pint of boiling sweet cream, and the rest of the stock. Let it be for a considerable time on the very eve of boiling, that it may thicken, but take care it does not boil, lest the cream curdle. Strain through a sieve.

I am also menaced in her letter with immediate marriage –of which I am equally unconscious – at

White soup is very old. A delicate veal broth (French *blond
de veau*), it was known in Scotland as *soup-à- la-reine* –
a relic of the Auld Alliance between that country and
France – and Byron probably tasted it first as a child in
Aberdeen. In its more elaborate version, Lorraine soup,
(the word is probably a corruption of *La Reine*) it
appeared frequently on fashionable dinner and
supper menus in Byron's day.

A VERY SUPPORTING BROTH
Against Any Kind of Weakness

Boil two pounds of loin of mutton, with a very large
handful of chervil, in two quarts of water. Take off
part of the fat. Any other herb or roots may be added.
Take half a pint three or four times a day.

SOUPE DE SANTE,
or *Au Naturel*

Take some broth well skimmed, and the fat taken off. Take thin slices of crust of bread, cut round, of the size of a shilling. Soak them separately in a little broth. As you are going to serve up, put the whole into a tureen without shaking, for fear of crumbling the bread, and make it thick; add some of the vegetables that have been boiled in the broth, and trimmed nicely.

This 'health' soup was popular in Byron's time in France and Italy, and it appears in the first course on the only surviving menu (a rough sketch on the back of a letter dated February 4th 1822) from the Pisan days when Byron held lavish weekly dinners for Shelley, and other friends.

My Lord is now living very sociably giving dinners for his male acquaintance and writing divinely.

MARY SHELLEY TO MRS GISBORNE,
DECEMBER 20th 1821

SAUCES

Traditionally the French have been dismissive of English cookery, not least in the sauce department, but in Byron's lifetime there was considerable French influence in the kitchens of polite society. Many great chefs were working in exile for the English aristocracy after the Revolution and it was becoming increasingly fashionable to employ a French cook and to take an intelligent interest in eating. Byron himself, clearly preferred the simpler, less pretentious traditional English cookery, though at the same time he hated *'the perpetual lamentations after beef and beer'* of the Englishman abroad, *'the stupid bigoted contempt of everything foreign.'* In Venice though, he found himself hankering after the piquancy of an English sauce to enliven the dreary Lenten fish dishes. That confusingly named sauce Melted Butter was the basis of many British sauces, but it has definite French connections. More like a *beurre blanc,* it could be mixed with flavoured vinegars, catsups, essences, pickled oysters and so on.

TO MELT BUTTER PLAIN,
or for sauces

Break the butter in small bits, and put it into a small saucepan, (kept for this and other delicate uses) with either cream, sweet milk, or water, or a mixture of them, in the proportion of a dessert-spoonful to the ounce of butter, Dredge fine wheat flour or potato-flour over this, and, holding the vessel over the fire, toss it quickly round, till the butter melts into the consistency of a very thick cream. Let it boil up and no more. This is sauce blanche. Some French cooks add a very little vinegar and nutmeg.

> *"He was a good man, sir, an excellent man; he had the best melted butter I ever tasted in my life"*.
> *EARL OF DUDLEY, ON A DECEASED BARON OF THE EXCHEQUER.*

ANOTHER WAY – Make a thick batter of flour with a wine-glassful of water, and six ounces of butter broken. Stir this quickly till it comes to the boiling point. Observe: A spoonful of catsup, and a little vinegar flavoured or plain converts this extempore into a good fish sauce; – a tea-spoonful of mustard, where suitable, will heighten the relish,

EGG SAUCE

Boil the eggs hard, and cut them into small pieces; then put them to melted butter.

OYSTER SAUCE

Save the liquor in opening the oysters; and boil it with the beards, a bit of mace, and lemon-peel. In the meantime throw the oysters into cold water, and drain it off. Strain the liquor, and put it into a sauce-pan with them, and as much butter, mixed with a little milk, as will make sauce enough; but first rub a little flour with it. Set them over the fire, and stir all the time; and when the butter has boiled once or twice, take them off, and keep the sauce- pan near the fire, but not on it; for if done too much, the oysters will be hard. Squeeze a little lemon juice, and serve.

If for company, a little cream is a great improvement. Observe, the oysters will thin the Sauce, so put butter accordingly. Cockles make excellent sauce done as above, observing to clear them from any sand that may be in the shells.

Although there is little mystery in the composition of oyster-sauce, like melted butter, it is rarely well made; it commonly resembles thick butter with lukewarm oysters in it.

LOBSTER SAUCE

Pound the spawn, and two anchovies; pour on them two spoonsful of gravy: strain all into some butter, melted as directed, then put in the meat of the lobster; give it all one boil, and add a squeeze of lemon.

ANOTHER WAY

Leave out the anchovies and gravy; and do it as above, either with or without a little salt and ketchup, as you like. Many prefer the flavour of the lobster and salt only.

SHRIMP SAUCE

If the shrimps are not picked at home, pour a little water over them to wash them; put them to butter melted thick and smooth: give them one boil, and add the juice of a lemon.

ANCHOVY SAUCE

Chop one or two anchovies without washing: put them to some flour and butter and a little drop of water: stir it over the fire till it boils once or twice. When the anchovies are good, they will be dissolved; and the colour and flavour much better than by the usual way.

WHITE SAUCE for BOILED FOWLS

Boil a large blade of mace, two cloves, and fifteen peppercorns, in half a pint of soft water, until the flavour be obtained: strain it off, put it into a saucepan with four anchovies chopped fine, a quarter of a pound of butter rolled in flour, and half a pint of cream. Boil, and stir well, two minutes. Put some in a tureen, and the remainder in the dish.

A SAUCE for ROAST FOWLS

Put into a small stew-pan two slices of ham, a clove of garlic, a laurel-leaf, and sliced onions: add a little good gravy, a sprig of knotted marjoram, and a spoonful of tarragon vinegar: simmer slowly an hour; strain off, and put into the dish or a boat.

SAUCE for FOWL of ANY SORT

Boil some veal-gravy, pepper, salt, the juice of a Seville orange and a lemon, and a quarter as much of port wine as of gravy and pour it into the dish or a boat.

SAUCE for COLD FOWL, or PARTRIDGE

Rub down in a mortar the yolks of two eggs boiled hard, an anchovy, two dessert-spoonsful of oil, three of vinegar, a shalot, Cayenne, if approved, and a teaspoonful of mustard. All should be pounded before the oil is added. Then strain it. Shalot-vinegar, instead of shalot, eats well; but then omit one spoonful of the common vinegar. Salt to your taste.

A VINAIGRETTE FOR COLD FOWL, OR MEAT

Chop mint, parsley, and shalot; mix with salt, oil and vinegar. Serve in a boat.

SAUCE for WILD FOWL

Simmer a tea-cupful of port wine, the same quantity of good meat gravy, a little shalot, a little pepper, salt, a grate of nutmeg, and a bit of mace, for ten minutes; put in a bit of butter and flour, give it all one boil, and pour it through the birds. In general they are not stuffed, but may be done so if liked.

APPLE SAUCE for GOOSE and ROAST PORK

Pare, core and slice some apples; and put them in a stone jar, into a saucepan of water, or on a hot hearth. If on a hearth, let a spoonful or two of water be put in, to hinder them from burning. When they are done, bruise them to a mash, and put to them a piece of butter the size of a nutmeg, and a little brown sugar. Serve in a sauce tureen.

AN EXCELLENT SAUCE for BOILED CARP, or TURKEY

Put half a pound of butter with a tea-spoonful of flour, put to it a little water, melt it, and add near a quarter of a pint of thick cream, and half an anchovy chopped fine, not washed, set it over the fire; and as it boils up, add a large spoonful of real India soy. If that does not give it a fine colour, put a little more. Turn it into the sauce-tureen, and put some salt and half a lemon: stir it well, to prevent its curdling.

(India Soy is difficult to purchase genuine: it should be made from an Indian plant called Dolichos sojah, or soya; but treacle and salt are the basis of the soy ordinarily sold).

GREEN SAUCE, for GREEN GEESE or DUCKLINGS

Mix a quarter of a pint of sorrel juice, a glass of white wine, some scalded gooseberries, some white sugar, and a bit of butter. Boil them up, and serve in a boat.

A SAUCE for DUCKS

Serve a rich gravy in the dish; cut the breast into slices, but do not take them off; cut a lemon, and put pepper and salt on it; then squeeze it on the breast, and pour a sponful of gravy over before you help.

CLEAR SHALOT SAUCE

Put a few chopped shalots into a little gravy, boiled clear, and near half as much vinegar: season with pepper and salt: boil half an hour.

(POOR MAN'S SAUCE is made by chopping a few shalots very fine, and warming them with a little pepper and salt, in vinegar and water. It is excellent with young roast turkey.)

SHELLFISH

I am very comfortable here – listening to that monologue of my father in law which he is pleased to call conversation-he has lately played once upon the fiddle – to my great refreshment – we have had visitors – & they are gone – I have got Kinnaird's receipt for the shellfish – but no shellfish for the receipt ... – Well – now I want for nothing but an heir to my estate – and an estate for my heir.

BYRON TO HOBHOUSE, MARCH 3rd 1815

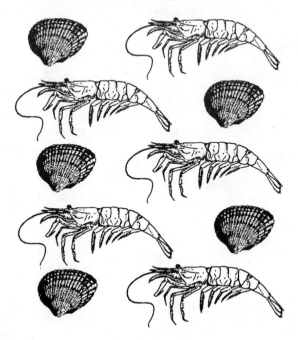

TO FEED OYSTERS

Put them in water, and wash them with a birch besom till quite clean; then lay them bottom-downwards into a pan, sprinkle with flour, or oatmeal and salt, and cover with water. Do the same every day, and they will soon fatten. The water should be pretty salt.

> While Venus fills the heart (without heart really
> Love, though good always, is not quite so good,)
> Ceres presents a plate of vermicelli, –
> For love must be sustain'd like flesh and blood,
> While Bacchus pours out wine, or hands a jelly:
> Eggs, oysters, too, are amatory food;
> But who is their purveyor from above
> Heaven knows, – it may be Neptune, Pan, or Jove

DON JUAN, CANTO II, clxx

Oysters were much more plentiful in Byron's day than they are now, and indeed were an ingredient of homely Lancashire Hotpot. So any 'amatory' qualities in them were not founded on their scarcity value. Perhaps Byron had personal experience to justify the claim. At any rate, he enjoyed eating them, and the recipe referred to, in his letter on the previous page, was for stewed oysters –

TO STEW OYSTERS

Open, and separate the liquor from them, then wash them from the grit; strain the liquor and put with the oysters a bit of mace and lemon-peel, and a few white peppers. Simmer them very gently, and put some cream, and a little flour and butter. Serve with sippets. The beards should be removed. They require very few minutes.

TO FRY OYSTERS

Take a quarter of a hundred of large oysters, beat the yolks of two eggs, add to it a little nutmeg, and a blade of mace pounded, a spoonful of flour and a little salt, dip in oysters, and fry them in hog's lard a light brown, if you choose you may add a little parsley shred fine. N.B. They are a proper garnish for cod's head, calf's head or most made dishes.

TO PICKLE OYSTERS

Wash four dozen of the largest oysters you can get in their own liquor, wipe dry, strain the liquor off, adding to it a dessert-spoonful of pepper, two blades of mace, a table-spoonful of salt (if the liquor be not very salt), three of white wine, and four of vinegar. Simmer the oysters a few minutes in the liquor, put them in small jars, then boil the pickle up, skim it, and when cold, pour over the oysters: cover close.

LOBSTER SALAD

Make a salad; and put some of the red part of the lobster to it, cut. This forms a pretty contrast to the white and green part of the vegetables. Do not put much oil, as the shell-fish absorb the sharpness of vinegar. Serve in a dish, not a bowl. Where salads are constantly used, if the ingredients are kept ready much trouble and time will be saved. The following proportions make a most excellent salad:

Four mustard ladles of mustard.

Four salt-ladles of salt.

Three dessert spoonful of essence of anchovies. Four ditto of the best mushroom-ketchup.

Three ditto of the best sweet oil.

Twelve ditto of vinegar, and
The yolks of three eggs boiled hard.
When the salad vegetables are cleaned, and put into
a bowl, pour over them a sufficient quantity of the
above, and stir it well.

I'm fond of fire, and crickets, and all that,
A lobster-salad, and champagne, and chat.

DON JUAN, CANTO I, cxxxv

... a woman should never be seen eating or drinking
unless it be lobster salad & champagne ...

BYRON TO LADY MELBOURNE

TO ROAST LOBSTERS

Half boil your lobster, rub it well with butter and set
it before the fire, baste it all over till the shell looks
a dark brown. Serve it up with a good Melted Butter.

BUTTERED LOBSTERS

Pick the meat out, cut it, and warm with a little weak
brown gravy, nutmeg, salt, pepper, and butter, with a
little flour. If done white, a little white gravy and
cream.

BOILED COCKLES

Cockles are delicious and nutritious, and may be eaten raw or cooked. You should however leave them for a few hours in clean sea water or fresh, salted water so that they can purge themselves before you cook them. Cover them with water, bring to the boil and boil for a few minutes only so that they don't toughen.

Last night I suffered horribly – from an indigestion, I believe. I never sup – that is, never at home. But, last night, I was prevailed upon by the Countess Gamba's persuasion, and the strenuous example of her brother, to swallow, at supper, a quantity of boiled cockles, and to dilute them, not reluctantly, with some Imola wine. When I came home apprehensive of the consequences, I swallowed three or four glasses of spirits, which men (the vendors) call brandy, rum, or Hollands, but which Gods would entitle spirits of wine, coloured or sugared. All was pretty well till I got to bed, when I became somewhat swollen, and considerably vertiginous. I got out, and mixing some soda-powders, drank them off. This brought on temporary relief. I returned to bed, but grew sick and sorry once and again. Took more soda-water. At last I fell into a dreary sleep. Woke, and was ill all day, till I had galloped a few miles. Query – was it the cockles, or what I took to correct them, that caused the commotion?

RAVENNA JOURNAL, FEBRUARY 27th, 1821

F I S H

Byron loved all fish. Sometimes he would give up meat for long periods – probably because he liked it too much and hated to be *"a slave of any appetite"*, but also because he believed that animal food *"engenders the appetite of the animal fed upon."* He instanced the manner in which boxers are fed as a proof, while, on the contrary, a regime of fish and vegetables served *"to support existence without pampering it."* This whim could sometimes cause inconvenience to his hosts and while staying with his parents-in-law at Seaham, Mrs. Clermont reports that *"He could live on nothing but fish & two grooms were constantly looking for it. He said he was starved."*

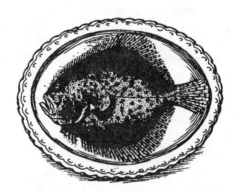

TO BOIL TURBOT

The turbot-kettle must be of a proper size, and in the nicest order. Set the dish in cold water sufficient to cover it completely, throw a handful of salt and a glass of vinegar into it, and let it gradually boil. When thick, the fish is apt to be unequally done; to prevent which, cut a slit down the back of two inches, close to the bone, and the same on the belly side, with a small sharp knife. Be very careful that there fall no blacks; but skim it well, and preserve the beauty of the colour. Serve it garnished with a complete fringe of curled parsley, lemon, and horse-radish. The sauce must be the finest lobster, anchovy butter, and plain butter, served plentifully in separate tureens.

If necessary, turbot will keep a couple of days, or more, in perfection, if a little salt be sprinkled over it, and it be hung in a very cool place.

On dismounting, found Lieutenant E. just arrived from Paenza. Invited him to dine with me tomorrow. Did not invite him for today, because there was a small turbot, (Friday, fast regularly and religiously,) which I wanted to eat all myself. Ate it.

RAVENNA JOURNAL, JANUARY 26th, 1821.

RED MULLET

It is called the sea-woodcock. Clean, but do not open or wash the inside, fold in oiled paper, and gently bake in a small dish. Make a sauce of the liquor that comes from the fish, with a piece of butter, a little flour, a little essence of anchovy, and a glass of sherry. Give it a boil; and serve in a boat, and the fish in the paper case it was dressed in.

STEWED CARP

Scale and clean, take care of the roe, etc. Lay the fish in a stew-pan, with a rich beef-gravy, an onion, eight cloves, a dessert-spoonful of Jamaica pepper, the same of black, a fourth part of the quantity of gravy of port (cider may do); simmer close covered; when nearly done, add two anchovies chopped fine, a dessert-spoonful of made mustard, some fine walnut ketchup, a bit of butter rolled in flour: shake it, and let the gravy boil a few minutes; add a spoonful of soy. Serve with sippets of fried bread, the roe fried, and a good deal of horseradish and lemon.

PERCH

Perch is a fish that is held in high estimation. Its flesh is white and delicate; the perch is easily digested, and is particularly recommended to those invalids who have a weak debilitated stomach.

Put them into cold water, boil them carefully, and serve with melted butter and soy. Perch are most delicate fish. They may be either fried or stewed: but in stewing they do not preserve so good a flavour.

COD'S HEAD and SHOULDERS

Will eat much finer by having a little salt rubbed down the bone, and along the thick part, even if it be eaten the same day. Tie it up, and put it on the fire in cold water which will completely cover it: throw a handful of salt into it. Great care must be taken to serve it without the smallest speck of black or scum. Garnish with a large quantity of double parsley, lemon, horseradish, and the milt, roe and liver, and fried smelts if approved. If with smelts, be careful that no water hangs about the fish; or the beauty of the smelts will be taken off, as well as their flavour. Serve with plenty of oyster or shrimp sauce, and anchovy and butter.

43

TO DRESS SALTED COD FISH

Cut in square bits, or put one large piece in water overnight; wash it clean in fresh water, and put on to boil in cold for one hour and a half; then cool the water, so that the fish may be easily handled; take it out of the saucepan and pick out the loose bones and scrape it clean without taking off the skin. Put it on in boiling water, and if the fish is too fresh add a little salt with it and let it boil gently from one hour to one and a half. The very thick part will take this time, the thin bits less, to dress. When dished, garnish with hard-boiled eggs and parsley.

Plain boiled parsnips and a butter tureen of egg sauce are served with it.

Byron appreciated salt fish of various kinds – which was as well for him as this was an important part of a Lenten or fast-day diet in Italy – particularly the dried salt cod known as *Baccalà*

TO FRY HERRINGS

After having cleansed your herrings, take out the roes, dry them and the herrings in a cloth. Flour them and fry them in butter of a fine brown. Lay them before the fire to drain. Slice three or four onions, flour them and fry them nicely. Dish up the herrings and garnish them with roes and onions. Send them up as hot as you can with butter and mustard in a boat.

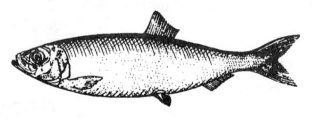

TO PICKLE HERRINGS

Take herrings, when washed, and put them into an earthen pot, with an onion, a few sweet herbs, lemon-peel, whole pepper, and as much vinegar and water as will cover them, of each an equal quantity; bake them one hour, in a slack oven, close covered with strong paper. – Keep them in the pickle.

I shall say nothing of Falmouth because I know it, & you don't, a very good reason for being silent as I can say nothing in its favour, or you hear anything, that would be agreeable. – The inhabitants both female & male, at least the young ones, are remarkably handsome, and how the devil they came to be so, is the marvel! For the place is apparently not favourable to Beauty.— The claret is good, and Quakers plentiful, so are Herrings salt & fresh ...

BYRON TO EDWARD ELLICE, JUNE 25th, 1809.

Fish Kettle & Slice.

POULTRY
& GAME

Byron often sent gifts of game to his friends, for instance, Leigh Hunt : *I send you some game of which I beg your acceptance – I specify the quantity as a security against the porter – a hare – a pheasant – and two brace of partridges which I hope are fresh. (OCTOBER 15th, 1814);* also to Robert Charles Dallas: *Dear Sir, – I send you three brace of birds two hares and a snipe, & apprise you before hand that you may neither be charged the carriage or wronged by Mr. Draper. (OCTOBER 14th, 1811).*

Sometimes Byron himself was given presents of game (venison in England and once in Italy a wild boar) which he distributed among friends in Pisa – including the Shelleys. On Byron's estate at Newstead game of all sorts was then plentiful, and many birds now extinct, or rare, and which we would not now consider eating, were consumed in large quantities. Byron enjoyed offering his sporting facilities to his friends, being not much interested in these himself.

The mellow autumn came, and with it came
The promised party to enjoy its sweets.
The corn is cut, the manor full of game;
The pointer ranges, and the sportsman beats
In russet jacket: – lynx-like is his aim;
Full grows his bag, and wonderful his feats,
Ah, nutbrown partridges! Ah, brilliant pheasants!
And ah, ye poachers: – 'Tis no sport for peasants.
DON JUAN, CANTO XIII, lxxv.

DUCKS, ROASTED

Stuff one with sage and onion, a dessert-spoonful of crums, a bit of butter, and pepper and salt; let the other be unseasoned. They should be done to a turn, and go up finely frothed, with a rich gravy in the dish.

I have found a temporary under-cook who is marvellously successful with trifles – ducks (without onions ...) and even with cakes – so I am not fasting.–

BYRON TO TERESA GUICCIOLI, JULY 17th, 1820.

ROAST PIGEONS

Roast pigeons should be stuffed with parsley, either cut or whole; and seasoned within. Serve with parsley and butter. Peas or asparagus should be dressed to eat with them.

Pigeons cropped up in Byron's household accounts in Greece, along with geese, capons, quails and woodcock.

TO ROAST GOOSE

After it is prepared, let it be well washed and dried, and a seasoning put in of onion, sage, and pepper and salt. Fasten it tight at the neck and rump, and then roast. Put it first at a distance from the fire, and by degrees draw it nearer. A slip of paper should be skewered on the breast-bone. Baste it very well. When the breast is rising, take out the paper; and be careful to serve it before the breast falls, or it will be spoiled by coming flatted to table. Let a good gravy be sent in the dish. Apple-sauce for a stubble goose, gooseberry sauce for a green one. A glass of port, a ladle of mustard, and some salt, put into the goose when the apron is cut off, give an additional flavour to the old goose.

> *Your friend Captain Medwin is at this moment with me ... The story in "Blackwood" (which I have only just heard) is utterly false. I have had no geese (not even one for Michaelmas Day), and I should neither be such a fool nor buffoon as to baptise them if I had.*

BYRON TO BRYAN WALLER PROCTER, 1822

But Byron did keep some geese later in 1822 at Pisa. Probably it meant a good deal to him in his days of exile to eat roast goose for Michaelmas because since the days of Elizabeth, roast goose stuffed with sage and onions was traditional fare for that day. She had been eating this, (a favourite dish) when news of the English victory over the Spanish Armada came to her, and so she enthusiastically declared that the occasion must be commemmorated every year on that day with the serving of roast goose.

TO KEEP GAME, &c.

Game ought not to be thrown away even when it has been kept a very long time; for when it seems to be spoiled, it may often be made fit for eating, by nicely cleaning it, and washing with vinegar and water. If there is danger of birds not keeping, draw, crop and pick them; then wash in two or three waters, and rub them with salt. Have ready a large saucepan of boiling water, and plunge them into it one by one; drawing them up and down by the legs, that the water may pass through them. Let them stay five or six minutes in; then hang them up in a cold place. When drained, pepper and salt the insides well. Before roasting, wash them well. The most delicate birds, even grouse, may be preserved thus. Those that live by suction cannot be done this way, as they are never drawn; and perhaps the heat might make then worse, as the water could not pass through them; but they bear being high. Lumps of charcoal put about birds and meat will preserve them from taint, and restore what is spoiling.

My dear Hay – I am really overpowered by your Caccia – which is too splendid – and I shall distribute it amongst my friends – with yr. remembrances. – I am sorry that I must decline my own proposition – and your kindness about the shooting at Bolgheri – as I have got a little world of business on my hands from England etc. – but I shall be more glad to see you again – than I could have been in any success in sporting.

BYRON TO JOHN HAY, FEBRUARY 6th, 1822.

PHEASANTS and PARTRIDGES

Roast them as turkey; and serve with a fine Gravy (into which put a very small bit of garlic), and bread-sauce. When cold, they may be made into excellent patties, but their flavour should not be overpowered by lemon.

GROUSE

Roast them like fowls, but the head is to be twisted under the wing. They must not be over-done. Serve with rich gravy in the dish, and bread-sauce. The sauce for wild fowl may be used instead of common gravy.

TO ROAST WILD FOWL

The flavour is best preserved without stuffing. Put pepper, salt, and a piece of butter, into each.

Wild fowl require much less dressing than tame; they should be served of a fine colour, and well frothed up. A rich brown gravy should be sent in the dish: and when the breast is cut into slices, before taking off the bone, a squeeze of lemon, with pepper and salt, is a great improvement to the flavour.

To take off the fishy taste which wild fowl sometimes have, put an onion, salt, and hot water into the dripping-pan, and baste them for the first ten minutes with this; then take away the pan, and baste constantly with butter.

WILD DUCKS

Should be taken up with the gravy in. Baste them with butter; and sprinkle a little salt before they are taken up, put a good gravy upon them, and serve with shalot-sauce in a boat.

WOODCOCKS, SNIPES, QUAILS

Keep good several days. Roast them without drawing, and serve on toast. Butter only should be eaten with them, as gravy takes off from the fine flavour. The thigh and back are esteemed the most. In helping, the lady must be careful to remove first a small bitter bag from the trail.

TO DRESS PLOVERS

Roast the green ones in the same way as woodcocks and quails (see above), without drawing; and serve on a toast. Gray plovers may be either roasted, or stewed with gravy, herbs and spice.

PLOVERS EGGS

A nice and fashionable dish. Boil them ten minutes, and serve either hot or cold; the former on a napkin, the latter on moss.

(Fresh green moss was often used in nineteenth century table decoration, mostly as a bedding for blossoms.)

HARES

If properly taken care of, will keep a considerable time, and even when the cook fancies them past eating may be in the highest perfection; which they cannot be if eaten when fresh killed. As they are usually paunched in the field, the cook cannot prevent this; but the hare keeps longer, and eats much better, if not opened for four or five days, or according to the weather.

If paunched, as soon as a hare comes in it should be wiped quite dry, the heart and liver taken out, and the liver scalded to keep for the stuffing. Repeat this wiping every day; mix pepper and ginger, and rub on the inside; and put a large piece of charcoal into it. If the spice is applied early, it will prevent that musty taste which long keeping in the damp occasions, and which also affects the stuffing.

An old hare should be kept as long as possible, if to be roasted. It must also be well soaked.

TO ROAST HARE

After it is skinned, let it be extremely well washed, and then soaked an hour or two in water; and if old, lard it; which will make it tender, as also will letting it lie in vinegar. If, however, it is put into vinegar, it should be exceedingly well washed in water afterwards. Put a large relishing stuffing into the belly, and then sew it up. Baste it well with milk till half-done, and afterwards with butter. If the blood has settled in the neck, soaking the part in warm water, and putting it to the fire warm, will remove it; especially if you also nick the skin here and there with a small knife to let it out. The hare should be kept at a distance from the fire at first. Serve with a fine froth, rich gravy, melted butter, and currant-jelly sauce; the gravy in the dish. For stuffing use the liver, an anchovy, some fat bacon, a little suet, herbs, pepper, salt, nutmeg, a little onion, crums of bread, and an egg to bind it all. The ears must be nicely cleaned and singed, and made crisp. They are reckoned a dainty.

TO JUG AN OLD HARE

After cleaning and skinning, cut it up; and season it with pepper, salt, allspice, pounded mace, and a little nutmeg. Put it into a jar with an onion, a clove or two, a bunch of sweet herbs, a piece of coarse beef, and the carcasse-bones over all. Tie the jar down with a bladder, and leather or strong paper; and put it into a saucepan of water up to the neck, but no higher. Keep the water boiling five hours. When it is to be served, boil the gravy up with a piece of butter and flour; and if the meat gets cold, warm it in this, but not to boil. Forcemeat balls may be served, but are not necessary.

TO POT A HARE
When the hare is skin'd; gutted and wash'd clean, cut it in pieces; put it in a stew-pot, with a pound and a half of butter, pepper and salt, nutmeg and mace, all beat fine; tie the top over with double paper, or put on a coarse paste; bake it for four hours; take out the meat; put into a mortar and beat it fine; if it wants more seasoning add it; then put it into the pot you would have it in, and press it down hard: pour clarified butter over it.

TO POT WOODCOCKS
Pluck and draw six woodcocks, skewer their bills through their thighs, put their legs through each other, and their feet on their breasts. Season with pepper, salt and mace. Put them into a deep pot, with a pound of butter on them. Bake them in a moderate oven, and not too much. Draw the gravy from them, then put them into potting-pots. Take all the clear butter from the gravy, and put it upon them. Fill up the pots with clarified butter. Keep them in a dry place. Snipes may be done in the same manner.

TO POT PARTRIDGES
Clean them nicely; and season with mace, allspice, white pepper, and salt, in fine powder. Rub every part

well; then lay the breast downwards in a pan, and pack the birds as close as you possibly can. Put a good deal of butter on them; then cover the pan with a coarse flour paste and a paper over, tie it close, and bake. When cold, put the birds into pots, and cover them with butter. The butter that has covered potted things will serve for basting, or for paste for meat pies.

TO MARINADE VENISON

Lay the meat in a covered dish, pour the following marinade over it, and leave for a day turning it from time to time.

Half a pint of red wine, half a pint of wine vinegar, half a pint of olive oil, twelve peppercorns, two bayleaves, a sliced onion, a sliced lemon, herbs, and a little salt.

TO DRESS VENISON

A haunch of buck will take three hours and a half or three quarters, roasting: doe only three hours and a quarter. Venison should be rather under than over done. Spread a sheet of white paper with butter, and put it over the fat, first sprinkling it with a little salt; then lay a coarse paste on strong paper, and cover the haunch; tie it with fine packthread, and set it at a distance from the fire, which must be a good one. Baste it often; ten minutes before serving take off the paste, draw the meat nearer the fire, and baste it with butter and a good deal of flour, to make it froth up well.

Gravy for it should be put into a boat, and not into the dish (unless there is none in the venison), and made thus: Cut off the fat from two or three pounds of a loin of old mutton, and set in steaks on a gridiron for a few minutes, just to brown one side; put them into a saucepan with a quart of water, cover quite close for an hour, and simmer it gently; then uncover it, and stew till the gravy is reduced to a pint. Season with salt only. Currant-jelly sauce must be served in a boat.

A HUFF PASTE FOR VENISON

Mix five pounds flour with ten ounces of lard and two pints of cold water gradually, to make a dough. This must be rested for thirty minutes before it is rolled out into an oblong shape a quarter of an inch thick, in which the joint will be enclosed. Several layers of paper well greased or steeped in olive oil are usually laid under the huff paste, with brown paper on top of it.

PERIGORD PIE

Make a forcemeat chiefly of green truffles, a small quantity of basil, thyme, parsley, knotted marjoram, the liver of any kind of game; if of woodcocks, that and the entrails, except the little bag, a small quantity of fat bacon, a few crumbs, the flesh of wild or tame fowls, pepper and salt. Lard the breasts of pheasants, partridges, woodcocks, moor-game, or whatever birds you have, with bacon of different sizes: cut the legs and wings from the backs, and divide the backs. Season them all with white pepper, a little Jamaica pepper, mace and salt. Make a thick raised crust to receive the above articles; it is thought better than a dish; but either will do. Line it closely with slices of fine, fresh, fat bacon; then cover it with stuffing; and put the different parts of the game lightly on it, with whole green truffles, and pieces of stuffing among and over it; observing not to crowd the articles, so as to cause them to be under-baked. Over the whole lay slices of fat bacon, and then a cover of thick common crust. Bake it slowly, according to the size of the pie, which will require a long time.

Some are made with a pheasant in the middle, whole; and the other game cut up and put around it.

I received, some time ago, a pâté de Périgord, and finding it excellent, I determined on sharing it with H(ill); but here my natural selfishness suggested that it would be wiser for me, who had so few dainties, to keep this for myself, than to give it to H(ill), who had so many. After half an hour's debate between selfishness and generosity, which do you think" (turning to me) "carried the point?" – I answered, "Generosity, of course". "No by Jove!" said he, "no such thing; selfishness in this case, as in most others, triumphed: I sent the pâté to my friend H(ill), because I felt another dinner of it would play the deuce with me; and so you see, after all, he owed the pâté more to selfishness than generosity.

LADY BLESSINGTON'S CONVERSATIONS OF LORD BYRON, ERNEST J. LOVELL, JR. 1969

MEAT

But man is a carnivorous production,
And must have meals, at least one meal a day;
He cannot live, like woodcocks, upon suction,
But like the shark and tiger, must have prey;
Although his anatomical construction
Bears vegetables, in a grumbling way
Your labouring people think beyond all question
Beef, veal, and mutton, better for digestion.

DON JUAN, CANTO II, lxvii

Byron loved beef, perhaps excessively: one reason why he often tried to do without it, becoming *"a leguminous-eating ascetic"* for months on end. This was no doubt easier in Italy, there being Fridays and Lent to observe, but also because beef was of poor quality : *"Dined – (damn this pen:) – beef tough – there's no beef in Italy worth a curse; unless a man could eat an old ox with the hide on, singed in the sun."*

(RAVENNA JOURNAL, JANUARY 24th, 1821).

So beef, and beef-steaks appear frequently in the exiled Byron's poetry – even as a cure for sea-sickness –

The best of remedies is a beef-steak
Against sea-sickness: try it, sir, before
You sneer, and I assure you this is true,
For I have found it answer – so may you.

DON JUAN, CANTO II, xiii

BEEF-STEAKS

Should be cut from a rump that has hung a few days. Broil them over a very clear or charcoal fire: put into the dish a little minced shalot, and a table-spoonful of ketchup; and rub a bit of butter on the steak the moment of serving. It should be turned often, that the gravy is not drawn out on either side.

This should be eaten so hot and fresh done, that it is not perfect if served with any thing else. Add pepper and salt when taking it off the fire.

> *And Juan too was helped out from his dream*
> *Or sleep, or whatso'er it was, by feeling*
> *A most prodigious appetite. The steam*
> *Of Zoe's cookery no doubt was stealing*
> *Upon his senses, and the kindling beam*
> *Of the new fire, which Zoe kept up, kneeling*
> *To stir her viands, made him quite awake*
> *And long for food, but chiefly a beefsteak.*
>
> *DON JUAN, CANTO II, cliii.*

> *For all we know that English people are*
> *Fed upon beef, I won't say much of beer,*
> *Because 'tis liqor only, and being far*
> *From this my subject, has no business here.*
> *We know too they are very fond of war,*
> *A pleasure, like all pleasures, rather dear;*
> *So were the Cretans, from which I infer*
> *That beef and battles both were owing to her.*
>
> *IBID, CANTO II, clvi.*

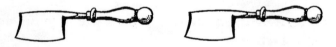

BEEF-STEAKS AND OYSTER SAUCE

Strain off the liquor from the oysters, and throw them into cold water to take off the grit, while you simmer the liquor with a bit of mace and lemon-peel; then put the oysters in; stew them a few minutes; add a little cream, if you have it, and some butter rubbed in a bit of flour; let them boil up once; and have rump-steaks, well seasoned and broiled, ready for throwing the oyster sauce over, the moment you are to serve.

ITALIAN BEEF-STEAKS

Cut a fine large steak from a rump that has been well hung, or it will do from any tender part: beat it, and season with pepper, salt, and onion; lay it in an iron stew-pan that has a cover to fit quite close, and set it by the side of the fire without water. Take care that it does not burn, but it must have a strong heat; in two or three hours it will be quite tender, and then serve, with its own gravy.

ROLLED BEEF-STEAKS

Beat some well-hung rump-steaks till tender, with a cleaver; make a forcemeat of the breast of a fowl, half a pound of veal, half the same sweetbread, all cut very small; a few truffles and morels stewed and cut, a shalot or two, some parsley, a little thyme, some grated lemon-peel, the yolks of two eggs, half a nutmeg, and a quarter of a pint of cream; mix these well together, and stir over the fire for ten minutes; lay the forcemeat on the steaks, roll them up, and skewer them tight; fry them a fine brown; take them from the fat, and stew them a quarter of an hour with a pint of beef-gravy, a spoonful of port, two ditto of ketchup, and a few fresh or pickled mushrooms. Take up the steaks, cut them in two, serve them with the cut side uppermost, and the gravy round, having carefully skimmed it. Garnish with lemon.

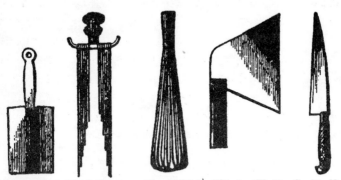

Cutlet Bat. Meat Skewers. Egg Whisk. Mincing Knife. Cook's Knife.

BEEF-STEAKS OF UNDERDONE MEAT

Cut them an inch and a half thick, with a good deal of fat; lay them on the gridiron over a quick fire, turn often, and as soon as brown lay them on a very hot dish that has been rubbed with shalot, and put in some of the gravy of the meat, and a spoonful of ketchup. When taken off the fire, put salt and pepper. If seasoned while broiling the meat will be hardened, and the juices wasted. The steaks may be served on chopped cabbage, warmed with butter, pepper and salt. Or the steaks as before, and the cabbage in a separate dish, with sliced fried potatoes round it.

BUBBLE AND SQUEAK

Cut some slices, not too thin, of cold boiled round or aitchbone of salt beef. Trim them neatly, as also an equal number of pieces of the white fat of the beef, and set them aside on a plate. Boil two summer or savoy cabbages, remove the stalks, chop them fine, and put them in a stewpan with four ounces of fresh butter and one ounce of glaze. Season with pepper and salt. When about to send to table, fry the slices of beef in a frying pan, commencing with the pieces of fat. Stir the cabbage on the fire until quite hot, and then pile it up in the centre of the dish. Place the slices of beef and the pieces of fat round it, pour a little thin brown sauce over the whole, and serve.

> *Alas! I must leave undescribed the gibier,*
> *The salmi, the consommé, the purée,*
> *All which I use to make my rhymes run glibber*
> *Than could roast beef in our rough John Bull way.*
> *I must not introduce even a spare rib here,*
> *"Bubble and Squeak" would spoil my liquid lay,*
> *But I have dined, and must forego, alas!*
> *The chaste description even of a "bécasse".*
>
> DON JUAN, CANTO XV, lxxi.

SWEETBREADS

For every mode of dressing, should be prepared ,by half-boiling, and then putting them in cold water. This, called blanching, makes them whiter and thicker, as well as firmer.

FRICASSEE of SWEETBREADS

Take five or six veal sweetbreads, according as you would have your dish in bigness, and boil them in water, cut them in thin slices the length way, dip them in egg, season with pepper and salt. Fry them a light brown. Then put them into a stewpan with a little brown gravy, a spoonful of white wine or juice of lemon, whatever you please. Thicken it up with flour and butter and serve it up. Garnish your dish with crisp parsley.

SWEETBREADS ROASTED

Parboil two large ones; when cold, lard them with bacon, and roast them in a Dutch oven. For sauce, plain butter and mushroom ketchup.

– As to Annabella she requires time & all the cardinal virtues, & in the interim I am a little verging towards one who demands neither, & saves me besides the trouble of marrying by being married already. – She besides does not speak English, & to me nothing but Italian, a great point, for from certain coincidences the very sound of that language is music to me, & she has black eyes & not a very white skin, & reminds me of many in the Archipelago I wished to forget, & makes me forget what I ought to remember, all which are against me. – I only wish she did not swallow so much supper,

chicken wings – sweetbreads, – custards – peaches & port wine – a woman should never be seen eating or drinking, unless it be lobster sallad & champagne, the only truly feminine & becoming viands.
BYRON TO LADY MELBOURNE,SEPTEMBER 25th, 1812.

LEG OF MUTTON

If roasted, serve to eat with it currant jelly, or onion sauce, salad, and potatoes.

MUTTON *à la* TURC

Wash it nicely in water, and then soak it in vinegar, and, without drying, put it into a stew-pan with a close cover, laying some skewers in the bottom to prevent the meat from sticking; put in a bunch of sweet herbs, three middling-sized onions, and as much water as you think will make the stew of a due consistence, a blade of mace, and a few peppercorns. Let it simmer very slowly. When the meat is very tender, take out the onions, herbs, add spice, and heat up in it an ounce of butter, and some salt.

ROAST LAMB with COCKLES

Make cuts all over the leg with a pointed knife and into each of these stuff a freshly-cooked shelled cockle rather as if the meat were larded with them. Roast it as usual and serve it garnished with horse- radish.

I dreamed last night of Ld. B. and I think my dream will not come true – it was that we were at dinner and that he eat voraciously of a Roasted Leg of Mutton, and said it was excellent. Joseph himself would be perplexed to expound this dream.

LADY MILBANKE TO ANNABELLA, 16th MARCH, 1815.

This was of course written during one of Byron's meat-less periods – he certainly *did* like mutton –

Today is the 9th. – and the l0th. is my surviving daughter's birthday – I have ordered as a regale a mutton chop and a bottle of Ale – she is seven years old I believe. Did I ever tell you that the day I came of age – I dined on eggs and bacon and a bottle of ale; for once in a way – they are my favourite dish & drinkable but as neither of them agree with me – I never use them but on great Jubilees once in four or five years or so.

BYRON TO JOHN MURRAY, DECEMBER 9th, 1822.

KNUCKLE OF VEAL

As few people like boiled veal, it may be well to make the knuckle small. Take off some cutlets or collops before it be dressed; and as the knuckle will keep longer than the fillet, do not cut off the slices till wanted. Break the bones to make it take less room; wash well, and put in a saucepan with three onions, a blade of mace or two, a few peppercorns; cover it with water, and simmer till ready. In the meantime some macaroni should be boiled with it if approved, or rice, or a little rice flour, to give it a small degree of thickness; but do not put too much. Before it is served, add half a pint of milk and cream, and let it come up either with or without the meat. The meat may be served in the soup, or on a separate dish. If the latter it may be covered with onion sauce. Bacon and some greens, are usually eaten with boiled veal. Put chopped parsley for garnish.

All went on very well yesterday and it appeared to me B. was particularly well last night. He complained of pain from his pills &c but upon my telling him that was quite right seemed satisfied & said he thought he was better – staid at home – no brandy – & said very seriously he should go to Kirkby in Feby. & that "they must keep us for 6 months." Of course I said nothing to discourage such a plan. I have seen him but a moment today when he was eating a stewed knuckle of Veal with broth & rice.

AUGUSTA TO ANNABELLA, 21st JANUARY, 1816.

RAGOUT of BREAST of VEAL

Half roast the best end of it. Flour it, stew it gently with three pints of good gravy, an onion, a few cloves and black pepper-corns, a bit of lemon-peel. Turn it whilst it stews, when very tender strain the sauce, if not thick enough mix a little more flour smooth. Add catchup, truffles, morels, mushrooms, boil it up; hard yolks of eggs.

That is to say, if your religion's Roman,
And you at Rome would do as Romans do,
According to the proverb, – although no man,
If foreign, is obliged to fast; and you,
If Protestant, or sickly, or a woman,
Would rather dine in sin on a ragout –
Dine and be d—d! I don't mean to be coarse,
But that's the penalty, to say no worse.

BEPPO, A VENETIAN STORY, IX.

A PILLOW OF VEAL

Half roast a neck or breast of veal. Cut it into pieces, and season it with pepper, salt and nutmeg. Take a pound of rice, and put to it a quart of broth, some mace and a little salt. Stew it over a stove on a very slow fire till it is thick, but butter the bottom of the pan in which you do it. Beat up the yolks of six eggs, and stir them into it. Take a little round deep dish, butter it, and lay some of the rice at the bottom: then put the veal in a round heap and cover it all over with rice. Rub it over with the yolks of eggs, and bake it an hour and a half. Open the top and pour in a pint of good rich gravy. Garnish with a seville orange cut in quarters and send it hot to table.

I cant find that he is any loss, being tolerably master of the Italian & modern Greek languages, which last I am also studying with a master, I can order and discourse more than enough for a reasonable man. – Besides the perpetual lamentations after beef & beer, the stupid bigotted contempt for everything foreign, and insurmountable incapacity of acquiring even a few words of any language, rendered him like all other English servants, an incumbrance. – I do assure you the plague of speaking for him, the comforts he required (more than myself by far) the pilaws (a Turkish dish of rice & meat) which he could not eat, the wines which he could not drink, the beds where he could not sleep, & the long list of calamities such as stumbling horses, want of tea!!!

&c. which assailed him, would have made a lasting source of laughter to a spectator, and of inconvenience to a Master.

BYRON TO MRS. CATHERINE GORDON BYRON, JAN 14th, 1811.

TO POT VEAL

Take part of a leg of veal, and put it in a pot with half a pound of butter, and lay a paste over it, and bake it in a moderate oven two hours; then take it out and cut off the out-sides, and put it in a marble mortar, and season it with salt, white pepper, and mace: pound it very fine, putting in the butter that is on the gravy, and have some more melted down, which you must put in by degrees; beat it to a fine paste, and put it down in pots, and the next day pour clarified butter over it.

TO COLLAR PIG'S HEAD

Scour the head and ears nicely; take off the hair and snout, and take out the eyes and the brain; leave in water one night; then drain, salt it extremely with common salt and saltpetre, and let lie five days. Boil to take out the bones; then lay on a dresser, turning the thick end of one side of the head to the thin end of the other, to make the roll of equal size; sprinkle with salt and white pepper, and roll it with the ears; and if you approve, put the pig's feet round the outside when boned or the thin parts of two cow-heels. Put into a cloth, bind with a broad tape, and boil it till quite tender; then put a good weight upon it, and do not take off the covering till cold.

If you choose it to be more like brawn, salt it longer, let the proportion of saltpetre be greater, and put in also some pieces of lean pork; and then cover it with cow-heel to look like the horn.

> *I have been out of town since Saturday & only returned last Night from my visit to Augusta. – I swallowed the D—l in ye shape of a collar of brawn one evening for supper (after an enormous dinner too) and it required all kinds of brandies & I don't know what besides to put me again in health & good humour – but I am now quite restored – & it is to avoid your congratulations upon fatness (which I abhor & you always inflict upon me after a return from the country) that I don't pay my respects to you today –*
>
> BYRON TO LADY MELBOURNE, APRIL 8th, 1814.

BOLOGNA SAUSAGES

Mince six pounds of rump of beef very fine, and two rounds of bacon; pound them; mix well with six or eight cloves of garlic; season it high with spices; fill it into very large hog-puddings, and tie them in nine-inch lengths; hang them in a dry warm place or in the smoke: they are eaten raw or boiled.

> *I'll tell you a story which is beastly – but will make you laugh; a young man at Ferrara detected his Sister amusing herself with a Bologna Sausage – he said nothing – but perceiving the same sausage presented at table – he got up – made it a low bow – and exclaimed "Vi riverisco mio Cognato." – Translate – and expound this to Scrope – and to "the Creature Dougal."*

BYRON TO JOHN CAM HOBHOUSE, VENICE, MAY 17, 1819.

The translation, by the way, is – "I pay my respects, brother-in-law". For hog-puddings, substitute sausage skins, which can be got nowadays in the animal or modern synthetic form.

COTECCHINO

50g black pepper (for 20 Kg meat and rind mixture).
30g salt for each Kg meat and rind
2 Kg leanish pork meat (shoulder or leg)
10 Kg pork rind
Sausage skins

Mince all thoroughly together, wash the skins, but not too vigorously, under the tap; fill them with the meat mixture, tie with string and hang up in a cold dry place for 3 or 4 months. Boil for 5 or 6 hours.

A New Year's dish in Italy, and one which appears on the only surviving menu from the days of grand entertaining at Pisa.

HAGGIS

Clean a sheep's pluck thoroughly. Make incisions in the heart and liver to allow the blood to flow out, and parboil the whole, letting the windpipe lie over the side of the pot to permit the discharge of impurities; the water may be changed after a few minutes boiling for fresh water. A half-hour's boiling will be sufficient, but throw back the half of the liver to boil till it will grate easily; take the heart, the half of the liver, and part of the lights, trimming away all skins and black-looking parts, and mince them together. Mince also a pound of good beef-suet and four or more onions. Grate the other half of the liver. Have a dozen of small onions peeled and scalded in two waters to mix with this mince. Have ready some finely ground oatmeal, toasted slowly before the fire for hours, till it is of a light brown colour and perfectly dry. Less than two teacupfuls of meal will do for this quantity of meat. Spread the mince on a board and strew the meal lightly over it, with a high seasoning of pepper, salt, and a little cayenne, first well mixed. Have a haggis bag (i.e. a sheep's paunch) perfectly clean, and see that there be no thin part in it, else your whole labour will be lost in bursting.

Some cooks use two bags, one as an outer case. Put in the meat with a half pint of good beef gravy, or as much strong broth as will make it a very thick stew. Be careful not to fill the bag too full, but allow the meat room to swell; add the juice of a lemon or a little good vinegar; press out the air and sew up the bag, prick it with a large needle when it first swells in the pot to prevent bursting; let it boil slowly for three hours if large.

"There are as good fish in the sea as ever came out of it." There is a Scotch proverb for you –
hot as haggis.
BYRON TO ALEXANDER SCOTT, JULY 31st, 1819.

Meat Chopper.

VINEGARS AND KETCHUPS

This feast is named the Carnival, which being
Interpreted; implies "farewell to flesh:"
So call'd, because the name and thing agreeing,
Through Lent they live on fish both salt and fresh.
But why they usher Lent with so much glee in
Is more than I can tell, although I guess
'Tis as we take a glass with friends at parting,
In the stage-coach or packet, just at starting.

And thus they bid farewell to carnal dishes,
And solid meats, and highly spiced ragouts
To live for forty days on ill-dress'd fishes,
Because they have no sauces to their stews;
A thing which causes many "poohs" and "pishes",
And several oaths (which would not suit the Muse)
From travellers accustom'd from a boy
To eat their salmon, at the least, with soy;

And therefore humbly I would recommend
"The curious in fish-sauce", before they cross
The sea, to bid their cook, or wife, or friend,
Walk or ride to the Strand, and buy in gross
(Or if set out beforehand, these may send
By any means least liable to loss),
Ketchup, Soy, Chili-vinegar, and Harvey,
Or, by the Lord! a Lent will well nigh starve ye;

BEPPO – A VENETIAN STORY VI – VIII.

COMMERCIAL SAUCES, CHUTNEYS AND KETCHUPS were already fairly common in Regency England and home-made ones much earlier. Byron was particularly fond of highly-spiced foods and his taste for vinegar was remarked on by many of his friends – particularly on the occasions when he would dine out in company only on potatoes mashed up on a plate with vinegar. Flavoured vinegars were popular at the time and were used for salads or for adding extra flavour to sauces.

RASPBERRY VINEGAR

Put a pound of fine fruit into a China bowl, and pour upon it a quart of the best white wine vinegar; next day strain the liquor on a pound of fresh raspberries; and the following day do the same, but do not squeeze the fruit, only drain the liquor as dry as you can from it.

CUCUMBER VINEGAR

Pare and slice fifteen large cucumbers, and put them in a stone jar, with three pints of vinegar, four large onions sliced, two or three shalots, a little garlic, two large spoonsful of salt, three tea-spoonsful of pepper, and half a tea-spoonful of Cayenne. After standing for four days, give the whole a boil; when cold, strain, and filter the liquor through paper. Keep in small bottles, to add to salad, or eat with meat.

SHALOT VINEGAR

Split six or eight shalots; put them into a quart bottle, and fill it up with vinegar; shake often; stop it, and in a month it will be fit for use.

To Make ELDER VINEGAR

Gather the elder flowers, when the sun is hot on them, and quite ripe, so that they will shake off the tree; fill a jug with them, and pour as much white wine vinegar in it as you can; set it in the sun for ten days; then strain it through a flannel bag, and bottle it.
(N.B. It will keep for seven years.)

To Make NASTURTIUM VINEGAR

Gather the buds of nasturtium flowers when small, put them into a bottle of white wine vinegar, and keep them in a warm dry place. A spoonful of this vinegar gives an agreeable flavour to fish sauce.

CAMP VINEGAR

Slice a large head of garlic; and put it into a wide-mouthed bottle, with half an ounce of Cayenne, two tea-spoonsful of real soy, two of walnut-ketchup, four anchovies chopped, a pint of vinegar, and enough cochineal to give it the colour of lavender-drops. Let it stand six weeks; then strain off quite clear, and keep in small bottles sealed up.

BASIL VINEGAR

Fill a wide-mouthed bottle with fresh green leaves of basil, and cover them with wine vinegar, and let them steep for 10 days. If you wish a very strong essence, Strain the liquor, put it on some fresh leaves, and let it steep fourteen days longer.

CHILLI VINEGAR

Cut half a pound of fresh chillis in halves and place in a covered jar, or bottle. Bring one pint of vinegar to the boil; leave until quite cold and pour over the chillies, then leave to infuse for a fortnight. Strain off the liquor, pour into bottles and cork tightly.

TO MAKE WHITE CATSUP
Take two quarts of white wine, a pint of elder-flower vinegar, a quart of water; put to them half a pound of anchovies and pickle, half a pound of horseradish, when scraped; one ounce of shalots, just bruised; one ounce of mace, a quarter of an ounce of nutmeg; boil it till half is consumed, then strain it, and when cold bottle it.

TO MAKE CUCUMBER CATSUP
Take six pounds of large cucumbers, when pared, put to them two pounds of onions sliced; cut the cucumbers very thin, and lay them in a deep pot, a layer of cucumbers and onions; put a good deal of salt on every layer; let them stand for two days; then break them well with your hands, and put them on a sieve to drain; to every quart of the liquor, put a quart of white wine, half a pound of anchovies, half an ounce of cloves and mace, some whole pepper, a little ginger, and horseradish scraped; boil all together for twenty minutes, then strain it, and when cold bottle it.

MUSHROOM CATSUP
After the mushrooms are wiped from the dust and dirt, slit them and put them into a pot, a layer of mushrooms, and a layer of salt; let them stand twelve hours; then boil them in the liquor a short time, and strain it from the mushrooms; and when it is cold, clear it from the sediment; the next day, give it

another boil or two, clearing it as before. The last time you boil them, to every quart of liquor, put half an ounce of spice to your liking, and a shalot; when cold, bottle it, and set it in a cool place, and it will keep for years.

PONTAC KETCHUP, for FISH

Put ripe elderberries, picked from the stalk, into a stone jar, with as much strong vinegar as will cover them. Bake with the bread; and, while hot, strain. Boil the liquor with a sufficient quantity of cloves, mace, peppercorns, and shalots, to give it a fine flavour. When that is obtained, put in half a pound of the finest anchovies to every quart of liquor; stir, and boil only until dissolved. When cold, put it into pint bottles, and tie double bladders over each cork. The same method should be observed for preserving all ketchups.

LEMON KETCHUP, or PICKLE

Cut three large juicy lemons across the top, and stuff salt into them; set them upright in a dish before the fire, and turn them every day. When they become dry, roast them in a Dutch oven until they are brown. Boil a quart of vinegar, with a quarter of a pound of anchovies, without the bones and scales (but do not wash them), four blades of mace, half a nutmeg sliced, and a spoonful of white pepper; boil gently ten minutes; then pour it, boiling hot, on the lemons, in a stone jar; and cover close. Let it stand six weeks, then put it into quarter-pint flat bottles. It is excellent for made dishes, and the lemon eats well.

COCKLE KETCHUP

Open the cockles, scald them in their own liquor; add a little water, when the liquor settles, if you have not enough; strain through a cloth, then season with every savoury spice; and if for brown sauce, add port, anchovies, and garlic – if for white, omit these, and put a glass of sherry, lemon-juice and peel, mace, nutmeg, and white pepper. If for brown, burn a bit of sugar for colouring. This is excellent in made dishes, or for fish sauce.

HARVEY SAUCE

One dozen of anchovies, six dessert-spoonsful of soy, ditto of good walnut pickle, three heads of garlic, two shalots, one ounce of Cayenne pepper, quarter of an ounce of cochineal, one gallon of vinegar. Cut the anchovies small but do not remove the bones. Chop the pickles, shalots and garlic then put all the ingredients into a deep jar and let it stand fourteen days, stirring it well two or three times every day. Then strain through a jelly-bag till it is quite clear, bottle it, (seal the corks with wax). A large spoonful of this stirred into a quarter-pint of thickened melted butter makes an admirable extemporaneous sauce.

CURRANT JELLY, Red or Black

Strip the fruit, and in a stone jar stew them in a saucepan of water, or by boiling it on the hot hearth; strain off the liquor, and to every pint weigh a round of loaf-sugar; put the latter in large lumps into it, in a stone or China vessel, till nearly dissolved; then put it in a preserving pan; simmer and skim as necessary. When it will jelly on a plate, put it in small jars or glasses.

SWEETS, CAKES & BISCUITS

Byron enjoyed sweet things and some-times permitted himself the odd indulgence. Trifles were popular then, both in England and in Italy, where they were known as *Zuppa Inglese* (English soup!), and so were custards, ice-creams and sorbets. Byron would often send for the latter to a local café and would allow himself the pleasure of eating them with Teresa in his garden in the hot summer months – sometimes as many as seven a day would be sent for.

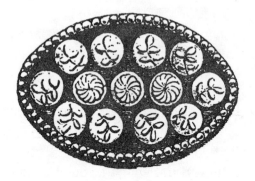

CURRANT OR RASPBERRY-WATER ICE

The juice of these, or any other sort of fruit, being gained by squeezing, sweetened, and mixed with water, will be ready for icing.

ICE CREAMS

To a pound of preserved fruit, of any kind, add a quart of cream, the juice of two lemons, to quicken the flavour, and sugar to your taste. Rub the whole through a fine hair sieve; and to raspberry, or any other red fruit, add a little cochineal colouring, to give a better tint.

BROWN BREAD ICE

Grate as fine as possible stale brown bread, soak a small proportion in cream two or three hours, sweeten, and ice it; but keep stirring, that the bread may not sink.

GINGER ICE CREAM

Take 4 oz of ginger preserved. Pound it and put it in a basin with two gills of syrup, a lemon squeezed and one 1 pint of cream; then freeze it.

AN EXCELLENT TRIFLE

Lay macaroons and ratafia-drops over the bottom of your dish, and pour in as much raisin-wine as they will suck up; which when they have done, pour on them cold rich custard, made with more eggs than directed in the following recipe, and some rice-flour. It must stand two or three inches thick; on that put a layer of raspberry jam, and cover the whole with a very high whip made the day before, of rich cream, the whites of two well beaten eggs, sugar, lemon-peel, and raisin-wine, well beat with a whisk, kept only to whip syllabubs and creams. If made the day before used, it has quite a different taste, and is solid and far better.

RICH CUSTARD

Boil a pint of milk with lemon-peel and cinnamon; mix a pint of cream, and the yolks of five eggs well beaten; when the milk tastes of the seasoning, sweeten it enough for the whole; pour it into the cream, stirring it well; then give the custard a simmer till of a proper thickness. Do not let it boil, stir the whole time one way; season as above. If to be extremely rich, put no milk, but a quart of cream to the eggs.

> *I have found a temporary under-cook who is marvellously successful with trifles ... and even with cakes.*
>
> *BYRON TO TERESA GUICCIOLI, JULY 17th, 1820.*

PRESERVED GINGER

Preserved ginger comes to us from the West Indies. It is made by scalding the roots when they are green and full of sap, then peeling them in cold water, and putting them into jars, with a rich syrup; in which state we receive them. It should be chosen of a bright-yellow colour, with a little transparency: what is dark-coloured and fibrous, and stringy, is not good. Ginger roots fit for preserving, and in equal size to West Indian, have been produced in the Royal Agricultural Garden in Edinburgh.

Lewis is going to Jamaica to suck his sugar-canes, he sails in two days; I enclose you his farewell note. I saw him last night at D(rury) L(ane) T(heatre) for the last time previous to his voyage. Poor fellow: he is really a good man – an excellent man – he left me his walking-stick and a pot of preserved ginger. I shall never eat the last without tears in my eyes; it is so hot.

BYRON TO THOMAS MOORE, NOVEMBER 4th, 1815.

PLUM PUDDING

Mix six ounces of suet, seven ounces of grated bread, two ounces of sugar, half a pound of French plums, three well-beaten eggs, a small tea-cup of milk, and a dessertspoonful of ratafia. Let it stand two hours, and boil it the same space of time. Observe to stir it well the last thing.

Dined versus six o' the clock. Forgot that there was a plum-pudding, (I have added, lately, eating to my "family of vices,") and had dined before I knew it. Drank half a bottle of some sort of spirits – probably

*spirits of wine; for what they call brandy, rum, &c
&c, here is nothing but spirits of wine, coloured
accordingly. Did not eat two apples which were
placed by way of dessert.*

RAVENNA JOURNAL, JANUARY 5th, 1821.

MINCE PIES

Of scraped beef or tongue, free from skin and strings,
weigh 2 lb., 4 lb. of suet picked and chopped, then add
6 lb. of currants nicely cleaned and perfecty dry, jar-
raisins stoned and chopped 2 lb., 3 lb. of chopped
apples, the peel and juice of two lemons, a pint of
sweet wine, a quarter of a pint of brandy, a nutmeg,
a quarter of an ounce of cloves, ditto mace, ditto
pimento, in finest powder; press the whole into a deep
pan when well mixed, and keep it covered in a dry
cool place.

Half the quantity is enough, unless for a very large
family.

Have citron, orange, and lemon-peel ready, and cut
some of each in the pies when made.

MINCE PIES WITHOUT MEAT

Of the best apples —six pounds, pared, cored,
and minced. Of fresh suet, and raisins stoned,
each three pounds, and likewise minced. To these
add of mace and cinnamon, a quarter of an
ounce each, and eight cloves, in finest powder,
three pounds of the finest powder sugar,
three quarters of an ounce of salt: the rinds
of four and juice of two lemons, half a
pint of port, the same of brandy.

Mix well, and put into a deep pan.

LEMON MINCE PIES

Squeeze a large lemon, boil the outside till tender enough to beat to a mash, add to it three large apples chopped, and four ounces of suet, half a pound of currants, four ounces of sugar; put the juice of the lemon and candied fruit, as for other pies. Make a short crust, and fill the pattypans as usual.

Dear Sir, – I have made a sumptuous meal on your minced pies –which were worthy of the donor and of his table. I congratulate you on your Cook. – Seven years have elapsed since I saw a minced pie – and time and distance had not diminished my regret for those absent friends to "a merry Christmas and a happy new year" – both of which I augur for you and your family, although the congratulation for the former is somewhat of the latest.

BYRON TO I. INGRAM, JANUARY 16th, 1823.

TO MAKE RICH GINGERBREAD

Rub a pound of butter into a pound of flour, grate in it the rind of a lemon; add half a pound of powder sugar, and two ounces of ground ginger; mix all well together and make it into a paste, with three quarters of a pound of treacle, and a glass of brandy, roll it thin, and bake it on tins in a cool oven.

GINGERBREAD, Another Sort

To three quarters of a pound of treacle beat one egg strained; mix four ounces of brown sugar, half an ounce of ginger sifted; of cloves, mace, allspice, and nutmeg: a quarter of an ounce, beaten as fine as possible; coriander and caraway seeds, each a quarter of an ounce; melt one pound of butter, and mix with the above; and add as much flour as will knead into a pretty stiff paste; then roll it out, and cut into cakes. Bake on tin plates in a quick oven. A little time will bake them.

Of some, drops may be made.

> *Caro il mio Pappa – Essendo tempo di Fiera desidererei tanto una Visita del mio Pappa, che ho' molte voglie da levarmi, non vorra compiacere la sua Allegrina che l' ho ama tanto?*
>
> *(My dear Papa – it being Fair time I should so much like a visit from my Papa, as I have many desires to satisfy, will you not please your Allegrina who loves you so?)*

Byron received this touching note from his illegitimate daughter Allegra who was a pupil at the Convent of Bagnacavallo (and where she died not long afterwards at the age of five).

He enclosed the note in a letter to Richard Belgrave Hoppner –

> *Apropos of the Epistles – I enclose you* two *– one from the Prioress of a Convent – & the other from my daughter her pupil – which is sincere enough but not very flattering – for she wants to see me because "it is the fair" to get some paternal Gingerbread – I suppose. –*

> SEPTEMBER 28th 1821.

A RICH PLUMB CAKE

Take one pound of butter, and beat it till it looks like cream; then take fourteen ounces of loaf sugar, pounded and sifted; the yolks of nine eggs, beat with three tablespoonfuls of rose water, and the same quantity of brandy, a whole nutmeg grated; beat these all well together, then add the whites of the eggs, heat to a froth, and one pound and quarter of fine flour, with two pounds of currants, cleaned and dried; three ounces of almonds blanched and sliced, and the same quantity of candied peel, cut in slices, beat it an hour; and it will take two hours baking.

TWELFTH CAKE

Two pounds of sifted flour, two pounds of sifted loaf sugar, two pounds of butter, eighteen eggs, four pounds of currants, one half pound of almonds, blanched and chopped, one half pound citron, one pound of candied orange and lemon peel, cut into thin slices, a large nutmeg grated, half an ounce ground allspice; ground cinnamon, mace, ginger, and corianders, a quarter of an ounce each, and a gill of brandy.

Put the butter into a stewpan, in a warm place, and work it into a smooth cream with the hand, and mix it with the sugar and spice in a pan (or on your paste board) for some time; then break in the eggs by degrees, and beat it at least twenty minutes; – stir in the brandy, and then the flour, and work it a little – add the fruit, sweetmeats, and almond, and mix all together lightly, – have ready a hoop cased with paper, on a baking plate, put in the mixture, smooth it on the top with your hand– dipped in milk. Put the plate on another, with sawdust between, to prevent the bottom from colouring too much – bake it in a slow oven four hours or more, and when nearly cold, ice it.

ICING FOR TWELFTH CAKE

Take one pound of double refined sugar, pounded and sifted through a lawn sieve; put into a pan quite free from grease, break in the whites of six eggs, and as much powder blue as will lie on a sixpence; beat it well with a spattle for ten minutes, then squeeze in the juice of a lemon, and beat it till it becomes thick and transparent. Set the cake you intend to ice in an oven for five minutes, then spread over the top and sides with the mixture as smooth as possible; if for a wedding cake only, plain ice it, if for a Twelfth Cake, ornament it with Paste and fancy articles of any description.

Observe: a good Twelfth Cake, not baked too much, and kept in a cool dry place, will retain its moisture and eat well, if twelve months old.

My dearest A – I shall write tomorrow – but did not go to Ly M(elbourne)'s twelfth cake banquet. M(ary Chaworth Musters) has written again – all friendship – & really very simple & pathetic – bad usage – paleness – ill health – old friendship – once – good motive – virtue – & so forth. — you shall hear from me tomorrow -

BYRON TO AUGUSTA, JANUARY 7th, 1814.

Twelfth night in Byron's day was celebrated somewhat like Christmas with social gatherings and special cakes. Usually the cake was decorated with candied fruits and a bean was put inside it as a token. Whoever found the bean became King or Queen for the day and various rituals were observed.

A BRIDE CAKE

Take four pounds of fine flour well dried, four pounds of fresh butter, two pounds of loaf sugar. Pound or sift fine a quarter of an ounce of mace, the same of nutmegs. To every pound of flour put eight eggs, with four pounds of currants: pick them well and dry them before the fire; blanch a pound of sweet almonds, and cut them lengthways very thin, a pound of citron, one pound of candied orange, the same of candied lemon, half a pint of brandy.

First work the butter with your hand to a cream, then beat in your sugar a quarter of an hour, beat the whites of your eggs to a very strong froth: mix them with your sugar butter; beat your yolk half an hour at least and mix them with your cake; then put in your flour mace and nutmeg. Keep beating until your oven is ready; put in your brandy, and beat your currants and almonds lightly in; tie three sheets of paper round the bottom of your hoops to keep from running out; rub it well with butter: put in your cake and lay your sweetmeats in three layers with cake betwixt every layer; after it is risen. It will take three hours in the baking.

TO MAKE ALMOND ICING for the BRIDE CAKE

Beat the whites of three eggs to a strong froth: beat a pound of Jordan almonds very fine with rose water. Mix your almonds with the eggs lightly together, a pound of loaf sugar beat very fine and put it in by degrees. When your cake is enough take it out and lay your icing on, then put it in to brown.

TO MAKE SUGAR ICING for BRIDE CAKE

Beat two pounds of double refined sugar with two ounces of fine starch. Sift it through a gauze sieve: then beat the whites of five eggs with a knife upon a pewter dish half an hour or it will make the eggs fall and will not be so good for colour: when you have put in all your sugar, beat half an hour longer then lay on your almond icing and spread it over with a knife: if it be put on as soon as the cake leaves the oven it will be hard by the time the cake is cold

"The Cake" dearest – I am in such agitation about it – if should be spoiled or mouldy – or – don't let them put too many eggs & butter in it – or it will certainly circulate an indigestion amongst all our acquaintance.

BYRON TO ANNABELLA MILBANKE,
DECEMBER 7th, 1814.

PLAIN AND VERY CRISP BISCUITS

Make a pound of flour, the yolk of an egg, and some milk, into a very stiff paste; beat it well, and knead till quite smooth; roll very thin, and cut into biscuits. Bake them in a slow oven till quite dry and crisp.

OLIVER'S BISCUITS

Mix a large spoonful of yeast in two spoonsful of new milk, add it to a pound and a half of flour, and let it rise half an hour. Melt two ounces of butter and half an ounce of white sugar in as much milk as shall make the flour into a dough. Roll it out thin, cut into biscuits, prick it well, and bake in a middling hot oven.

Hobhouse writes me a facetious letter about my indolence – and love of Slumber. – It becomes him – he is in active life – he writes pamphlets against Canning to which he does not put his name – he gets into Newgate – and into Parliament – both honourable places of refuge – and he "greatly daring dines" at all the taverns – (why didn't he set up a tap room at once?) and then writes to quiz my laziness. – Why I do like one or two vices to be sure – but I can back a horse and fire a pistol without "winking or blinking" like Major Sturgeon – I have fed at times for two months together on sheer biscuit & water (without metaphor) I can get over seventy or eighty miles a day riding post and swim five at a Stretch taking a piece before & after as at Venice in 1818 or at least I could do & have done (it) once & I never was ten minutes in my life over a solitary dinner.

BYRON TO JOHN MURRAY, OCTOBER 9th, 1820.

Byron regularly reverted to a favourite diet of tea and dry biscuits *("six per diem")* when he wanted to lose weight or to discipline himself; and sometimes he would soak them in vinegar as he did potatoes. In Italy he ate *ciamelletti biscottati,* but in England the usual plain biscuits were the type popularised by Dr. Oliver of Bath.

BEVERAGES

Now Laura moves along the joyous crowd,
Smiles in her eyes, and simpers on her lips;
To some she whispers, others speaks aloud;
To some she curtsies, and to some she dips,
Complains of warmth, and this complaint avow'd,
Her lover brings the lemonade, she sips;
She then surveys, condemns, but pities still
Her dearest friends for being dress'd so ill.
> *BEPPO, A VENETIAN STORY, lxv.*

In the evenings I do one of many nothings – either at the theatres, or some of the conversaziones, which are like our routs, or rather worse, for the women sit in a semicircle by the lady of the mansion, and the men stand about the room. To be sure, there is one improvement upon ours – instead of lemonade with their ices, they hand about stiff rum-punch – punch, by my palate; and this they think English. I would not disabuse them of so agreeable an error, – "no, not for Venice."
> *BYRON TO THOMAS MOORE,*
> *DECEMBER 24th, 1816.*

But Byron did enjoy lemonade in the heat of the Italian summer, at any rate he frequently sent for it to a local café along with sorbets and sometimes coffee.

LEMONADE
to be Made a Day Before Wanted
Pare two dozen tolerably sized lemons as thin as possible, put eight of the rinds into three quarts of hot, not boiling water, and cover it over for three or four hours. Rub some fine sugar on the lemons to attract the essence, and put it into a China bowl, into which squeeze the juice of the lemons. To it add one pound and a half of fine sugar, then put the water. to the above, and three quarts of milk made boiling hot; mix, and pour through a jelly-bag till perfectly clear.

LEMONADE Another Way
Pare a number of lemons according to the quantity you are likely to want; on the peels pour hot water, but more juice will be necessary than you need use the peels of. While infusing, boil sugar and water to a good syrup with the white of an egg whipt up; when it boils pour a little cold water into it; set it on again, and when it boils up, take the pan off, and set it to settle. If there is any scum, take it off, and pour it clear from the sediment to the water the peels were infused in, and the lemon-juice, stir and taste it: and add as much more water as shall be necessary to make a very rich lemonade. Wet a jelly-bag, and squeeze it dry, then strain the liquor, which is uncommonly fine.

ICE WATERS
Rub some fine sugar on lemon or orange, to give the colour and flavour, then squeeze the juice of either on its respective peel; add water and sugar to make a fine sherbet, and strain it before it be put into the ice-pot. If orange, the greater proportion should be of

the China juice, and only a little of Seville, and a small bit of the peel grated by the sugar.

BARLEY WATER

Wash common or pearl barley, and take in the proportion of an ounce to a quart of water. Give it a boil for a few minutes in a very little water, and strain off this, and take fresh water, which will make the barley water lighter and of a better colour. Boil it down one half. Lemon peel and sugar may be added, or a compound draught made, by adding to every pint of the decoction an ounce of stoned raisins, a quarter ounce of sliced liquorice root and three or four figs. With lemon juice it is less cloying and more grateful to the sick, Currant jelly answers very well in barley water.

I have been very ill with a slow fever, which at last took to flying, and became as quick as need be. But, at length, after a week of half-delirium, burning skin, thirst, hot headache, horrible pulsation, and no sleep, by the blessing of barley water, and refusing to see any physician, I recovered. It is an epidemic of the place, which is annual, and visits strangers.

... I have now written you at least six letters, or letterets, and all I have received in return is a note about the length you used to write from Bury Street to St. James's-street, when we used to dine with Rogers, and talk laxly, and go to parties, and hear poor Sheridan now and then. Do you remember one night he was so tipsy, that I was forced to put his cocked hat on for him – for he could not, – and I let him down at Brookes's, much as he

must since have been let down into his grave. Heigh
ho! I wish I was drunk – but I have nothing but this
d—d barley-water before me.

BYRON TO THOMAS MOORE, MARCH 25th, 1817.

TO MAKE The Celebrated Eastern
BEVERAGE, called SHERBET

This liquor is a species of negus without the wine. It
consists of water, lemon or orange juice, and sugar, in
which are dissolved perfumed cakes, made of the best
Damascus fruit, and containing also an infusion of some
drops of rose-water: another kind is made of violets,
honey, juice of raisins, etc. It is well calculated for
assuaging thirst, as the acidity is agreeably blended with
sweetness. It resembles indeed, those fruits which we
find so grateful when one is thirsty.

– but don't ask me to alter for I can't – I am obstinate
and lazy – and there's the truth. – But nevertheless
– I will answer your friend C.V. who objects to the
quick succession of fun and gravity – as if in that
case the gravity did not (in intention at least)
heighten the fun. – His metaphor is that "we are
never scorched and drenched at the same time!"
– Blessings on his experience! Ask him these
questions about "scorching and drenching". –
Did he never play at Cricket or walk a mile in hot
weather? – did he never spill a dish of tea over his
testicles in handing the cup to his charmer to the
great shame of his nankeen breeches? – did he never
swim in the sea at Noonday with the Sun in his eyes
and on his head – which all the foam of ocean could
not cool? did he never draw his foot out of a tub of
too hot water damning his eyes & his valet's? did

*he never inject for a Gonorrhea? or make water
through an ulcerated Urethra? Was he ever in a
Turkish bath – that marble paradise of sherbet and
sodomy? –*

BYRON TO JOHN MURRAY, AUGUST 12th, 1819.

Byron probably first came across Sherbets on his travels
in Turkey although they had been appearing in English
Cookery books for some time.

*He told me to consider him as a father whilst I was
in Turkey & said he looked on me as his son. –
Indeed he treated me like a child, sending me almonds & sugared sherbet, fruit & sweetmeats 20
times a day. – He begged me to visit him often and
at night when he was more at leisure – I then after
coffee & pipes retired for the first time. I saw him
thrice afterwards. – It is singular that the Turks who
have no hereditary dignities & few great families
except the Sultan's pay so much respect to birth, for
I found my pedigree more regarded than even my
title.*

*BYRON TO MRS. CATHERINE GORDON BYRON,
NOV.12th, 1809.*

*The beverage was various sherbets
Of raisin, orange, and pomegranite juice,
Squeez' d through the rind, which makes it best for use.*

DON JUAN, CANTO III, lxii.

ICE PUNCH, as used in Italy
Make a rich sherbet, and grate a piece of sugar on a
lemon or citron for flavour; then beat the whites of
five or six eggs to a froth, and by degrees stir it into
the sherbet: add rum and ice, and serve in glasses.

An EXCELLENT METHOD of MAKING PUNCH

Take two large fresh lemons with rough skins, quite ripe, and some large lumps of double-refined sugar. Rub the sugar over the lemons till it has absorbed all the yellow part of the skins. Then put into the bowl these lumps, and as much more as the juice of the lemons may be supposed to require; for no certain weight can be mentioned, as the acidity of a lemon cannot be known till tried, and therefore this must be determined by the taste. Then squeeze the lemon-juice upon the sugar; and with a bruiser press the sugar and the juice particularly well together, for a great deal of the richness and fine flavour of the punch depends on this rubbing and mixing process being thoroughly performed. Then mix this up very well with boiling water (soft water is best) till the whole is rather cool. When this mixture (which is now called the sherbet) is to your taste, take brandy and rum in equal quantities, and put them to it, mixing the whole well together again. The quantity of liquor must be according to your taste: two good lemons are generally enough to make four quarts of punch, including a quart of liquor, with half a pound of sugar; but this depends much on taste, and on the strength of the spirit.

As the pulp is disagreeable to some persons, the sherbet may be strained before the liquor is put in. Some strain the lemon before they put it to the sugar, which is improper; as when the pulp and sugar are well mixed together, it adds much to the richness of the punch.

When only rum is used, about half a pint of porter will soften the punch; and even when both rum and brandy are used, the porter gives a richness, and to some a very pleasant flavour. This receipt has never been in print before, but is greatly admired amongst the writer's friends. It is impossible to take too much pains in all the processes of mixing, and, in minding to do them extremely well, that all the different articles may be most thoroughly incorporated together.

I am but just returned to town, from which you may infer that I have been out of it; and I have been boxing, for exercise, with Jackson for this last month daily. I have also been drinking, – and, on one occasion, with three other friends at the Cocoa Tree, from six till four, yea, unto five in the matin. We clareted and champagned till two – then supped, and finished with a kind of regency punch composed of madeira, brandy, and green tea, no real water being admitted therein. There was a night for you! – without once quitting the table, except to ambulate home, which I did alone, and in utter contempt of a hackney-coach and my own vis, both of which were deemed necessary for our conveyance. And so, – I am very well, and they say it will hurt my constitution.

BYRON TO THOMAS MOORE, APRIL 9th, 1814.

SUMMER GIN PUNCH

is thus made at the Garrick Club: pour half a pint of gin on the outer peel of a lemon, then a little lemon-juice, a glass of maraschino, a pint and a quarter of water, and two bottles of iced soda-water; and the result will be three pints of the punch in question.

(Gin was about 52% alcohol in the early 19th century).

CHERRY BRANDY

Weigh the finest morellas, having cut off half the stalk; prick them with a new needle, and drop them into a jar or wide-mouth bottle. Pound three quarters the weight of sugar or white candy; strew over; fill up with brandy, and tie a bladder over.

> *Have you cleansed my pistols? and dined with the*
> *"Gineral"? My compts. to the Church of St. Johns,*
> *and peace to the ashes of Ball. – How is the Skipper?*
> *I have drank his cherry brandy, and his rum has*
> *floated over half the Morea. – Plaudite et Valete.*
>
> BYRON TO JOHN CAM HOBHOUSE, JULY 29th, 1810.

HOCK AND SODA WATER

Hock and soda water is now popularly known as *spritzer*:

> *Man being reasonable must get drunk;*
> *The best of life is but intoxication.*
> *Glory, the grape, love, gold, in these are sunk*
> *The hopes of all men and of every nation;*
> *Without their sap, how branchless were the trunk*
> *Of life's strange tree, so fruitful on occasion.*
> *But to return. Get very drunk; and when*
> *You wake with headache, you shall see what then.*
>
> *Ring for your valet, bid him quickly bring*
> *Some hock and soda water, then you'll know*
> *A pleasure worthy Xerxes the great king;*
> *For not the best sherbet sublimed with snow,*
> *Nor the first sparkle of the desert spring,*
> *Nor Burgundy in all its sunset glow,*
> *After long travel, ennui, love, or slaughter,*
> *Vie with that draught of hock and soda water.*
>
> DON JUAN, CANTO II, clxxx, clxxxi.

Soda-water is the simplest stimulating liquid. To permanently weak stomachs it is generally unwholesome. It is always unwholesome during a meal, but is an excellent beverage at some interval afterwards.

TEA AND COFFEE

Byron appreciated teas of various sorts – indeed he was a friend of that Lord Grey (the 2nd) whose portrait we see today on those packets of bergamot-scented tea which bear his name (Earl Grey). Green tea crops up from time to time in the poetry, and while on starvation diet he would wash down his dry biscuits with this.

Here I must leave him, for I grow pathetic
Moved by the Chinese nymph of tears, green tea!
Than whom Cassandra was not more prophetic;
For if my pure libations exceed three
I feel my heart become so sympathetic,
That I must have recourse to black Bohea:
'Tis pity wine should be so deleterious,
For tea and coffee leave us much more serious.

  DON JUAN, CANTO IV , lii.

TO MAKE COFFEE

Put two ounces of fresh-ground coffee, of the best quality, into a coffee-pot, and pour eight coffee-cups of boiling water on it; let it boil six minutes, pour out a cupful two or three times, and return it again; then put two or three isinglass-chips into it, and pour one large spoonful of boiling water on it; boil it five minutes more, and set the pot by the fire to keep hot for ten minutes, and you will have coffee of a beautiful clearness. Fine cream should always be served with coffee, and either pounded sugar-candy, or fine Lisbon sugar.

If for foreigners, or those who like it extremely strong, make only eight dishes from three ounces. If not fresh roasted, lay it before a fire until perfectly hot and dry; or you may put the smallest bit of fresh butter into a preserving-pan of a small size, and, when hot, throw the coffee in it, and toss it about until it be freshened, letting it be cold before ground.

Byron had decided views (as he had on most culinary matters) on how coffee should be made. He appreciated most foods and drinks in their pure and unadulterated state and especially towards the end of his life when he lived very simply indeed – harking back nostalgically in his poetry to the unpretentious repasts of his youthful travels –

The simple olives, best allies of wine,
Must I pass over in my bill of fare?
I must, although a favourite "plat" of mine
In Spain, and Lucca, Athens, everywhere:
On them and bread 'twas oft my luck to dine,

The grass my table-cloth, in open air,
On Sunium or Hymettus, like Diogenes,
Of whom half my philosophy the progeny is.
                    DON JUAN, CANTO XV, lxxiii.

There is too, Don Juan's idyllic first breakfast with
Haidee on the shore of the island –

... But Zoe the meantime some eggs was frying,
Since, after all, no doubt the youthful pair
Must breakfast, and betimes – lest they should ask it
She drew out her provision from the basket.

She knew that the best feelings must have victual,
And that a shipwreck'd youth would hungry be;
Besides, being less in love, she yawn'd a little,
And felt her veins chill'd by the neighbouring sea;
And so, she cooked their breakfast to a tittle;
I can't say that she gave them any tea,
But there were eggs, fruit, coffee, bread, fish, honey
With Scio wine, – and all for love, not money.
                    DON JUAN, CANTO II, cxliv–cxlv.

Later came the elaborate repast *(The dinner made
about a hundred dishes)* warning that the idyll was
not to last for ever –

... And Mocha's berry, from Arabia pure,
In small fine coffee cups, came in at last;
Gold cups of filigree made to secure
The hand from burning underneath them placed,
Cloves, cinnamon, and saffron too were boil'd
Up with the coffee, which (I think) they spoil'd.
                    DON JUAN, CANTO III, lxiii.

BREAKFAST BEVERAGE

Byron frequently breakfasted on a raw egg – usually standing, it is reported. The following recipe comes from Mrs. Rundell's *Domestic Cookery* with which he was familiar –

An egg broken into a cup of tea, or beaten and mixed with a basin of milk, makes a breakfast more supporting than tea solely.

VARIOUS
RECEIPTS

But now at thirty years my hair is grey
(I wonder what it will be like at forty?
I thought of a peruke the other day);
My heart is not much greener, and in short I
Have squandered my whole summer while 'twas May,
And feel no more the spirit to retort. I
Have spent my life, both interest and principal,
And deem not, what I deemed, my soul invincible.

DON JUAN,CANTO I, ccxiii.

AN EXCELLENT WATER TO PREVENT HAIR FROM FALLING OFF, AND TO THICKEN IT

Put four pounds of unadulterated honey into a still, with twelve handsful of the tendrils of vines, and the same quantity of rosemary-tops. Distil as cool and as slowly as possible. The liquor may be allowed to drop till it begins to taste sour.

POMADE DIVINE

Clear a pound and a half of beef-marrow from the strings and bone, put it into an earthen pan, or vessel of water fresh from the spring, and change the water night and morning for ten days; then steep it in rose-water twenty-four hours; and drain it in a cloth till quite dry. Take an ounce of each of the following articles, namely, storax, gum-benjamin, odiferous cypress-powder, or of Florence, half an ounce of cinnamon, two drams of cloves, and two drams of nutmeg, all finely powdered; mix them with the marrow above prepared; then put all the ingredients into a pewter pot, that holds three pints; make a paste of white of egg and flour, and lay it upon a piece of rag. Over that must be another piece of linen to cover the top of the pot very close, that none of the steam may evaporate. Put the pot into a large copper pot, with water, observing to keep it steady, that it may not reach to the covering of the pot that holds the marrow. As the water shrinks, add more, boiling hot; for it must boil four hours without ceasing a moment.

Strain the ointment through a linen cloth into small pots, and, when cold, cover them. Do not touch it with any thing but silver. It will keep many years.

A fine pomatum may be made by putting half a pound of fresh marrow, prepared as above, and two ounces of hog's-lard, on the ingredients; and then observing the same process as above.

HARD POMATUM

Prepare equal quantities of beef-marrow and mutton-suet as before, using the brandy to preserve it, and adding the scent; then pour it into moulds, or, if you have none, into phials of the size you choose the rolls to be. When cold, break the bottles, clear away the glass carefully, and put paper round the rolls.

> *– my personal charms have by no means increased – my hair is half grey – and the Crow's-foot has been rather lavish of its indelible steps. – My hair though not gone seems going – and my teeth remain by way of courtesy – but I suppose they will follow – having been too good to last. –I have now been as candid as anything but a too faithful Mirror can be – I shall not venture to look in mine – for fear of adding to the list of that which Time has (added) – and is adding.*
>
> *BYRON TO JAMES WEDDERBURN WEBSTER,*
> *JULY 2nd, 1819.*

Byron was acutely conscious of his appearance, and his concern to keep his hair and teeth intact amounted almost to an obsession –

> *What's that you say about "yolk of egg for the hair"? The receipt – the receipt immediately.*
>
> *BYRON TO DOUGLAS KINNAIRD,*
> *APRIL 26th, 1821.*

I am not very well – having had a bilious pain in my Stomachic region for some days. – But I rides & jumbles it off as well as I can – with exercise & raw eggs. – By the way your hair receipt costs me an egg a day. – Does it nourish as well as embellish the hair?

POT POURRI

Put into a large china jar the following ingredients in layers, with bay-salt strewed between the layers: two pecks of damask roses, part in buds and part blown; violets, orange-flowers, and jasmine, a handful of each; orris-root sliced, benjamin, and storax, two ounces of each; a quarter of an ounce of musk; a quarter of a pound of angelica-root sliced; a quart of the red parts of clove-gillyflowers; two handsful of lavendar-flowers; half a handful of rosemary-flowers; bay and laurel leaves, half a handful of each; three Seville oranges, stuck as full of cloves as possible, dried in a cool oven, and pounded; half a handful of knotted marjoram, and two handsful of balm of Gilead dried. Cover all quite close. When the pot is uncovered, the perfume is very fine.

A Quicker Sort of SWEET POT

Take three handsful of orange-flowers, three of clove-gillyflowers, three of damask roses, one of knotted marjoram, one of lemon-thyme, six bay-leaves, a handful of rosemary, one of myrtle, half one of mint, one of lavendar, the rind of a lemon, and a quarter of an ounce of cloves. Chop all; and put them in layers, with pounded bay-salt between, up to the top of the jar.

If all the ingredients cannot be got at once, put them in as you get them; always throwing in salt with every new article.

...I have just been scolding my monkey for tearing the seal of her letter, and spoiling a mock book, in which I put rose leaves.

BYRON TO THOMAS MOORE, MAY 24th, 1820.

"Rose leaves", in Byron's day were in fact petals, and no doubt Byron saved them from Teresa's gifts, dried them and kept them with other mementos – as was the pleasant practice of the time – locks of hair, portraits, trinkets of various sorts, and, more macabre, in Teresa's case, a piece of Lord Byron's blistered skin which she had saved when he had been badly sunburned while swimming.

Thank you from my heart for the roses. Love me – my soul is like the leaves that fall in autumn – all yellow – A cantata!

BYRON TO TERESA GUICCIOLI,
SEPTEMBER 28th, 1820.

THE DINNER
from
CANTO XV
of
DON JUAN

THE VERSES

lxiii

There was a goodly "soupe à la bonne femme,"
Though God knows whence it came from; there was, too,
A turbot for relief of those who cram,
Relieved with "dindon à la Parigeux:"
There also was – the sinner that I am!
How shall I get this gourmand stanza through? –
"Soupe à la Beauveau," whose relief was dory,
Relieved itself by pork, for greater glory.

lxiv

But I must crowd all into one grand mess
Or mass; for should I stretch into detail,
My Muse would run much more into excess,
Than when some squeamish people deem her frail;
But though a "bonne vivante", I must confess
Her stomach's not her peccant part; this tale
However doth require some slight refection,
Just to relieve her spirits from dejection.

lxv

Fowls "à la Conde," slices eke of salmon,
With "sauces Genevoises," and haunch of venison:
Wines too, which might again have slain young Ammon—
A man like whom I hope we sha'n't see many soon;
They also set a glazed Westphalian ham on,
Whereon Apicius would bestow his benison;
And then there was champagne with foaming whirls,
As white as Cleopatra's melted pearls.

lxvi

Then there was God knows what "à l'Allemande,"
"A l'Espagnole," "timballe," and "salpicon" –
With things I can't withstand or understand,
Though swallowed with much zest upon the whole;
And "entremets" to piddle with at hand
Gently to lull down the subsiding soul;
With great Lucullus' Robe triumphal muffles –
(There's fame) – young partridge fillets, deck'd with truffles.

lxvii

What are the fillets on the victor's brow
To these? They are rags or dust.Where is the arch
Which nodded to the nation's spoils below?
Where the triumphal chariots' haughty march?
Gone to where victories must like dinners go
Farther I shall not follow the research:
But oh! ye modern heroes with your cartridges,
When will your names lend lustre e'en to partridges?

lxviii

Those truffles too are no bad accessaries,
Follow'd by "petits puits d'amour" – a dish
Of which perhaps the cookery rather varies,
So every one may dress it to his wish,
According to the best of dictionaries,
Which encyclopedise both flesh and fish;
But even sans "confitures," it no less true is,
There's pretty picking in those "petits puits."

lxix

The mind is lost in mighty contemplation
Of intellect expanded on two courses;
And indigestion's grand multiplication
Requires arithmetic beyond my forces.
Who would suppose, from Adam's simple ration,
That cookery could have call'd forth such resources,
As form a science and a nomenclature
From out the commonest demands of nature?

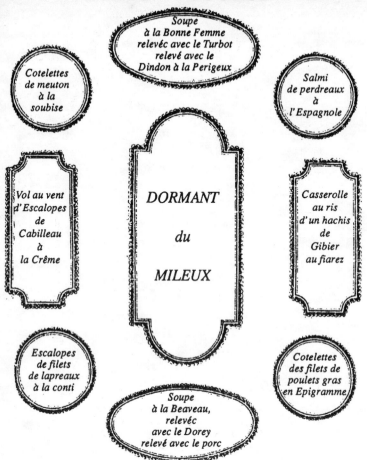

Soupe
à la Bonne Femme
relevéc avec le Turbot
relevé avec le
Dindon à la Perigeux

Cotelettes
de meuton
à la
soubise

Salmi
de perdreaux
à
l'Espagnole

Vol au vent
d'Escalopes
de
Cabilleau
à
la Crême

DORMANT

du

MILEUX

Casserolle
au ris
d'un hachis
de
Gibier
au fiarez

Escalopes
de filets
de lapreaux
à la conti

Cotelettes
des filets de
poulets gras
en Epigramme

Soupe
à la Beaveau,
relevéc
avec le Dorey
relevé avec le porc

Dinners in Byron's day consisted of two main courses and a desert. Each course would have several different dishes – soups, fish, meats and vegetables – laid out all at once in a formal pattern on the table. Guests would help themselves to whatever they wanted, and servants would change the plates as necessary: *And let the guests assist one another. Among the practises which interfere with*

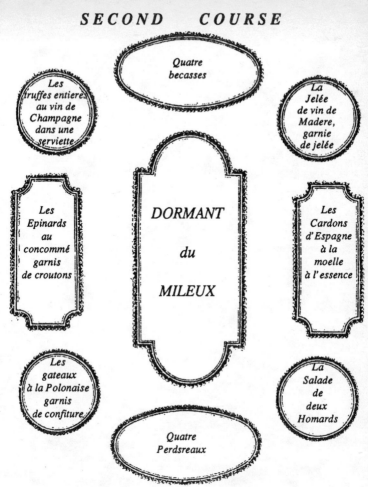

Quatre becasses

Les truffes entieres au vin de Champagne dans une serviette

La Jelée de vin de Madere, garnie de jelée

Les Epinards au concommé garnis de croutons

DORMANT

du

MILEUX

Les Cardons d'Espagne à la moelle à l'essence

Les gateaux à la Polonaise garnis de confiture

La Salade de deux Homards

Quatre Perdsreaux

helping wine to the company — said Eustace Ude. After the first course was removed, another of equal size and variety with perhaps even more elaborate meat dishes, would be brought in, and the guests would start again! Quantity – an accepted convention of hospitality – was staggering, the waste appalling, and the food became badly disfigured by the guests. Dessert consisted of sweet

MENU

SOUPE A LA BONNE FEMME
LE POTAGE A LA BEAUVEAU

LE TURBOT, SAUCE AU HOMARD
LE DOREY GARNI D'EPERLANS FRITS
LE SAUMON A LA GENEVOISE

LES POULARDES A LA CONDE
LE DINDIN A LA PERIGUEUX
LES FILETS DE PERDREAUX SAUTES
A LA LUCULLUS

LE JAMBON DE WESTPHALIE A L'ESSENCE
LE CUISSEAU DE PORC A DEMI SEL,
GARNI DE CHOUX
HAUNCHE DE VENAISON

PETITS PUITS D'AMOUR, GARNIS DE
CONFITURES

LES GLACES

LES FRUITS

On the frequent occasions when his command of English fails Ude lapses into French. Here is a short glossary of French terms he most uses.

à l'écarlate: in the scarlet manner

beurre d'anchois: anchovy butter

bouillon: stock

contre noix: the opposite end of the *noix* (see *sous noix* below)

coulis: liquid purée or thick sauce made from vegetables or shellfish

filet mignon: cut of beef

fricandeaux: meat balls

grand bouillon: very rich stock

liquor of braize: gravy from braised meat

mark, marquer: to brown

marmite: cooking pot or casserole

mouillez: moisten

parures: trimmings

puits d'amour: 'little wells of love'

quenelles: small lightly poached dumplings of spiced meat or fish forcemeat

rasp: grate, crumble by rubbing

sauce blanche: white sauce

sous noix: the *noix* is the fleshy upper part of the fillet end of a leg of veal. *Sous noix* is the drier, leaner portion below this.

tammy: rough woollen cloth (for straining)

We have been unable to define some terms (*cavice,* for example) which seem obsolete as well as French, since they are not to be found in the Larousse Encyclopedia Gastronomique.

SOUPE à la BONNE-FEMME

Take two handfuls of sorrel; after having taken off the stalks put the leaves one above another and mince them. Take the hearts of two or three cabbage-lettuces, which mince likewise. Wash the whole well, then take about two ounces of fresh butter, and let your herbs melt as it were, in the butter. When so, moisten with a little broth, and let it boil for an hour. Skim off the grease, and throw in a little sugar, to take off the acidity of the sorrel. Then thicken your soup with the yolks of eight eggs, mixed with a little cream. Be mindful to keep a little broth for the bread to soak in, for this could not be accomplished in broth when thickened.

POTAGE à la BEAUVEAU

Take some turnips, peel them, and use a cutter with which you cut out a few balls as round as possible, but very small. Blanch them, and boil them in some consommé, (see below) well clarified, with a little sugar. Serve up with bits of bread as in No.1, (see Soupe de Santé, p. 26) soak singly, not to spoil the look of the soup, which must appear very bright, and put to it two spoon-fuls of *blond de veau*.

GRAND CONSOMME

Mark in a marmite a large piece of small round of beef, with a knuckle of veal, and the other bones of the leg, according to the quantity of sauce you may want to make. Put likewise the parures of a neck of veal. This marmite will admit all manner of veal or poultry. Let the meat sweat over a gentle fire. *Mouillez* with about two large ladles full of *grand bouillon;* put no other vegetables in this *marmite,* except a bunch of parsley and green onions. Let them sweat thoroughly; then thrust your knife into the meat; if no blood issues it is a sign that it is heated through. Then moisten it with boiling *grand bouillon,* and let it boil for about four hours. You use this consommé to mark the sauces, or the consommés of either poultry or game. Skim off the grease and scum of all the various marmites, and keep them full, in order that the broth should not be too high in colour.

LE TURBOT à L'EAU SEL, SAUCE au HOMARD

Take a turbot that has disgorged, put it into boiling water, with a little salt, vinegar, or lemon juice. It must not be left in the water above three quarters of an hour. Then drain it, and send it up with the sauce separately. Lobster sauce is to be made as follows.

Take a hen lobster, cut the flesh into small dice, keep the eggs, which pound and strain through a hair sieve, after having mixed a little butter. You then make a *sauce blanche,* let it be rather thick: then mix the eggs of the lobster with that sauce, throw into it a little *beurre d'anchois,* a small quantity of cavice, a little cream. Take care the sauce does not boil, for it would curdle and lose colour.

LE JOHN DOREY,
SAUCE au HOMARD

Boil in the same manner as you do turbot. Send it up garnished with fried smelts.

LA SAUCE au BEURRE, DITE
SAUCE BLANCHE

According to the French way, we mark in a stewpan with a spoonful of flour, half a pound of fresh butter, a little salt, half a gill or glass of water, half a spoonful of white vinegar, and a little grated nutmeg. This sauce we put on the fire, when it begins to grow thick, for we do not allow it to boil, for fear it should taste of the flour. Serve up.

According to the English way, you mark in a stew-pan with a little flour, a small quantity of water, and a little butter: when the butter is melted, without having boiled, you send up.

TO FRY SMELTS

They should not be washed more than is necessary to clean them. Dry them in a cloth; then lightly flour them, but shake it off. Dip them into plenty of egg, then into bread crums grated fine, and plunge them into a good pan of boiling lard; let them continue gently boiling, and in a few minutes they will become a bright yellow-brown.

Take care not to take off the light roughness of the crums, or their beauty will be lost.

SALMON à la GENEVOISE

Take a few shalots, some roots of parsley, a bunch ditto seasoned with spices, thyme, bay-leaves, and a few carrots. Let the whole be lightly fried in a little butter. Then moisten with white wine (Madeira in preference). Let it boil for three-quarters of an hour. When the marinade is done, drain it through a tammy, over the fish, which stew in that seasoning. As soon as the fish is sufficiently stewed, drain it: pick it well of all the scales, and return it into the vessel wherein it has boiled, with some of the liquor to keep it hot. Now reduce some of the marinade with a good Espagnole (see below), skim all the fat or grease off, into which throw a good piece of butter. To be well kneaded with flour, a little *beurre d'anchois* (see below), all which will serve over the salmon after having drained it. Some will have lemon-juice to it, which is a matter of taste.

GRANDE ESPAGNOLE

Besides a little ham, mark in a stew-pan some pieces of veal, those parts namely that are called *sous noix* and *contre noix*. *Mouillez* the same as for the *coulis;* sweat them in the like manner; let all the glace go to the bottom, and when of a nice red colour, *mouillez* with a few spoonfuls of consommé to detach the glace: you then pour in the *coulis*. Let the whole boil for half an hour, that you may be enabled to remove all the grease. Drain it through a clean tammy. Remember always to put into your sauce some mushrooms, with a bunch of parsley and green onions.

LE BEURRE d' ANCHOIS

To make this sauce you must have young anchovies. Take them out of the pickling, wash them well. Take off the bones and head: then pound them in a mortar with fresh butter, till very fine: then rub the *beurre* through a hair sieve; put it in a cold place, and use it occasionally.

FOWLS à la CONDE

Take a couple of fine white fowls, empty them, take off the bone of the breast, and the nerves of the legs, then truss them, and introduce within the body a little butter seasoned with lemon juice and salt, which will make the fowls look well and whiter. Next mark them in a stew-pan trimmed with layers of bacon, cover them well and pour over them a *poële*, which is made in the following manner. Take a pound of veal, cut into dice, the same as a pound of fat bacon, and a little ham. Fry the whole white in half a pound of butter. Moisten the whole with pale broth, season with a bunch of parsley, salt, and pepper, and when sufficiently stewed drain it through a hair sieve over the fowls, which stew for three-quarters of an hour over a slow fire, but keep a brisk fire on the cover of the stew-pan. When done drain them, next dish them with a tongue *à l'écarlate* in the middle, and the sauce à la financière.

RAGOUT à la FINANCIERE

You must procure cock's combs, cock's kidneys, fat livers, likewise a few eggs of fowls. The combs are to be scalded in the following manner. Put the whole of them in a towel with a handful of salt, that has not been pounded. Then lay hold of the four corners of the towel, and dip the part wherein is the ragoût into boiling hot water. Leave it there for a minute. Then take out the towel. Rub the whole well together, to take off the first skin that is about the combs, and spread your towel open; if the combs be not skinned sufficiently, dip them into the boiling water a second time; but mind they do not get too firm, because then they never would get white. When they are well skinned, *parez* the little black points, that the blood may disgorge. Next dip them into a pint of water, and lay them on the corner of your stove for two hours; yet mind that there is but a very little fire in the said stove. You next blanch them; and put them in a little *blanc,* by which is meant butter, salt, water, and slice of lemon. Try them frequently with a wooden spoon, lest they should be too much done. The kidneys are not to boil, for then they would break. The eggs are to boil a little, in order that the first skin may come off. Now throw the whole into the *blanc*. As soon as the combs are done, you have ready a nice *Espagnole* reduced, with large mushrooms *tournée,* some small quenelles, which have been poached separately. Mix the whole together; drain the ragout, the combs, the kidneys, and the eggs. Put the whole in the sauce with the quenelles; stir gently, not to break the latter, season well, and use this sauce occasionally.

TURKEY à la PERIGUEUX

Take a nice fat turkey. The moment it has been killed, empty it, and put plenty of salt inside of the body. Then let it cool, and prepare some truffles in the following manner. Take a large quantity, peel them, and smell whether they be all of a good flavour. Then pick out the smallest, which chop very fine. Take some fat white bacon, and rasp it so as to procure the fat only without the nerves. When you have thus rasped a sufficient quantity to fill the body of the turkey, stuff the turkey with the chopped truffles and bacon seasoned with salt, spices, pepper, and cayenne-pepper, well mixed together. Sow the turkey up, and keep it in the larder for about a fortnight, so long as it retains a fine flavour. Then roast it well, wrapt up in layers of bacon and covered with paper, &c. Serve up with a *purée* of chestnuts *à brun*.

PUREE de MARONS

Take some fine new chestnuts; slit the peel with your knife, and put a little butter in a frying pan. Fry the chestnuts till the peel comes off; you then boil them in a little *consommé* and sugar. When done, add four or six spoonfuls of *Espagnole*, and rub the whole through a tammy. Keep this sauce rather liquid, as it is liable to go thick.

SAUCE à la LUCULLUS

Lucullus was one of the most renowned Epicures of ancient Rome; it is very natural of course to allot the name of a man who has brought the art of cookery into so high a repute, to a sauce which requires so much pains, attention, and science in the Art, and which can only be sent up to the table of a wealthy and true connoisseur.

When you are going to send up the dinner, *sautez* or fry gently the truffles, and when done drain the butter off: put them separately into a small stew-pan with a little essence of game and truffles. As you are to mask those parts only which are not decorated, take up the fillets and dip them into the sauce, but no deeper than the part which you have glazed slightly, in order to render the truffles blacker. When you have dished a large fillet and a small one alternately, you mask the *filets mignons* with the remainder of the sauce, and put in the middle the truffles, cut to the size of a penny, which have been lying in a sauce like that which has been used for the fillets.

When this sauce is made with great care, it is undoubtedly the *ne plus ultra* of the art.

CONSOMME OF GAME

If you are to send up entrées of partridges, you must have prepared a *consommé* of partridges. Mark in a stew-pan a few slices of veal, the backs, &c of partridges to be laid over. If you *mouillez* with a *consommé* containing ham, there is no occasion to put in any more; if not, a few slices of ham will not be amiss. If your *entrées* are *aux truffes,* add the *parures* of your truffles and a few mushrooms. When your *consommé* is sufficiently done, drain it through a cloth, or silk sieve, and use it when you have an opportunity.

WESTPHALIA HAM à l'ESSENCE

Take a small Westphalia ham, and trim it well. Be particular in sawing off the knuckle in order not to break the bone into splinters. Keep it a couple of days in water to take out the brine, and boil it in plain water for four hours. When done drain it, and take off the rind, then give it a nice round form. You then put it in the oven for a few minutes to dry the fat; which otherwise could not be glazed properly. When quite dried, glaze it of a fine colour, and serve under it an essence.

LA GLACE

The *glace* is very seldom made on purpose, except upon particular occasions. Then you lay on the fire a *marmite,* with plenty of veal and small quantity of beef and of ham. When stewed for a proper time skim it well. The *glace* of sweated broth is not so bright. Season the broth with carrots and onions; a large bunch of parsley and green onions; for either turnips or celery give the glace a bitter taste. If you should happen to have a grand dinner, and that you would wish to glaze of a nice colour, put more veal in your *Espagnole.* The moment it glazes, take part of the glace in a small stew-pan, which is only to serve for the purpose of glazing. The most common glace is made of remnants of broth, the liquor of *braize,* or *fricandeaux,* &c. which are to be reduced on a brisk fire. If you keep your reductions too long, they will become black and bitter. Always warm your glace *au bain marie,* that it may not get too brown.

LEG OF PORK

Take the leg of a porket, which rub over with salt, and put it well covered with salt also in a vessel, where it is to be left ten days. Then boil it in water and send it up with green cabbage all round, and a pease-pudding, which is made as follows.

Take a quart of dry peas, wash them clean, wrap them up in a clean towel and throw them in the same vessel as the leg. When the peas are done, strain them through a sieve, put in a good lump of butter, two eggs, and poach them, wrapped up in a clean towel, to make the pudding.

THE HAUNCH OF VENISON

It was customary in France to cut off a small rosette from the leg and to lard it, then to pickle it. In England it is the common way to lay it on the spit, then to make some paste with flour and water only, and to wrap the venison into that paste, which is secured by a few sheets of paper. It cannot be done thoroughly in less than four hours. It is usually served up with red currant-jelly made hot with a little port wine.

PUITS D'AMOUR GARNISHED WITH JAM

Spread some puff-paste, a foot square, and three-eighths of an inch thick. Have a small cutter, cut about two dozen; brush a *plafond* over with a little *dorure,* and put those small pasties on it, pressing on each of them with your finger: then brush each of them over with the *dorure*; open the little mark in the centre with a knife, and bake them quickly in a hot oven. When done, sift some pounded sugar over them, and glaze them very bright. Take out the crumb in the middle, and put the pasties on a clean sheet of paper, to draw off the butter. Garnish with different coloured sweetmeats, as cherry and apricot jam. (*Dorure* is an egg beaten up, yolk and white together.)

Notes for The Dinner from Canto XV of *Don Juan*

Byron was clearly familiar with the most popular cook books of his day. Indeed one of his publisher's (John Murray) great successes was Mrs. Rundell's *A New System of Domestic Cookery* (1806) which ran into about 70 editions and of which 5-10 thousand were published yearly. Byron was delighted to be associated with Mrs. Rundell in a commercial sort of way, though no doubt her straightforward, no-nonsense approach to cookery appealed to him as well.

> *The same illustrious Edinburgh bookseller (William Blackwood) once sent an order for books, poesy, and cookery, with this agreeable postscript – "The Harold and Cookery are much wanted." Such is fame, and, after all, quite as good as any other "life in others' breath." 'Tis much the same to divide purchasers with Hannah Glasse or Hannah More.*

– Hannah Glasse being the author of another immensely successful recipe book, *The Art of Cookery made Plain and Easy* (1747) which was still being reprinted nearly a hundred years later. This, too, was an extremely practical and unpretentious book – intended for the use of ordinary servants rather than for chefs in great houses –

> *If I have not wrote in the high polite Stile, I hope I shall be forgiven; for my intention is to instruct the lower sort; and therefore must treat them in their own way ... in many Things in cookery, the great cooks have such a high way of expressing themselves that the poor girls are at a loss to know what they mean ...*

Mrs. Glasse was highly critical of fancy foreign food and of the accompanying malpractises –

If gentlemen will have french cooks they must pay for French tricks. A Frenchman in his own country would dress a fine dinner of twenty dishes and all genteel and pretty for the expense he will put an English Lord to for dressing one dish ... So much is the blind folly of this Age that would rather be imposed on by a French booby than give encouragement to a good English cook.

Such sentiments no doubt appealed to Byron, and it comes as no surprise to learn that when he came to describe the Dinner in Canto XV of *Don Juan,* he didn't simply rely on personal memories of elaborate dinners in English Town and Country Houses, but he very deliberately consulted a suitably pretentious contemporary French cook book.

All the specified dishes in this dinner (stanzas lxiii – lxviii quoted above) come from *The French Cook* (1813) by Louis Eustache Ude, where they appear in suggested Bills of Fare for the months of November or December and for December or January. (There are accompanying Plates to show the proper arrangement of the dishes on the Table.)

The mind is lost in mighty contemplation
Of intellect expanded on two courses;
And indigestion's grand multiplication
Requires arithmetic beyond my forces.
Who would suppose, from Adam's simple ration,
That cookery could have call'd forth such resources,
As form a science and a nomenclature
From out the commonest demands of nature?

        DON JUAN, CANTO XV, lxix.

Byron's days of gourmandising were truly over by now and his wish was *"to live as simply as need be – for some years – though not sordidly."* He was declining most dinner and supper invitations, his diet was spartan, and he frequently harked back to the unpretentious pleasures of his youthful travels –

> *The simple olives, best allies of wine,*
> *Must I pass over in my bill of fare?*
> *I must, although a favourite "plat" of mine,*
> *In Spain, and Lucca, Athens, everywhere:*
> *On them and bread 'twas oft my luck to dine,*
> *The grass my table-cloth, in open air …*

> *DON JUAN, XV, lxxiii.*

– and so in the description of the dinner there is no nostalgia for the luxurious banquets of the England days, but a feeling of repugnance at memories of self-indulgence and gorging (*"a turbot for relief of those who cram"*) and a barely-concealed disgust at the sheer quantity of food. Any form of excess was now abhorrent to him, and not only because of the physical disgust he now habitually felt, but also because he wished to economise –

> *I should like (God willing) to leave something to my*
> *relatives more than a mere good name; and besides*
> *that to be able to do good to others to a greater*
> *extent. If nothing else will do – I must try bread &*
> *water – which by the way – are very nourishing –*
> *and sufficient – if good of their kind.*

> *LETTER TO DOUGLAS KINNAIRD, JANUARY 18th, 1823.*

It is unlikely therefore, that Ude's book was ever used in Byron's household; perhaps it had been brought there by one of his cooks, or lent by his last and dearest love, Teresa Guiccioli, but he had clearly read the Preface, where he found the Bills of Fare, and a Tone (echoed in stanza lxix) quite suited to his purpose –

> *Yes, if you Adopt and attend to the rules that I have laid down, the self-love of mankind will consent at last that Cookery shall rank in the class of the sciences, and its Professors deserve the name of artists*

And in the recipes he found all the 'tumult' and 'masquerade' he could have wished for.

But there was another side to Ude too, which came out more emphatically in a later edition of the book, after Byron's death. He was a highly sensitive emigré Frenchman with a gigantic chip on his shoulder, and one cannot help feeling some sympathy for him when he writes

> *after ten years of the utmost exertion to bring his Art to perfection, he (a head cook in England) ranks no higher than an humble domestic.*

Ude, who styled himself *"ci-devant chef to Louis XVI"* came to England after the Revolution and worked for the Earl of Sefton, then for the Duke of York, then as maitre d'hotel at various London Clubs. He was acutely sensitive to any criticism of his art, particularly when it was blamed for the high incidence of gout among the upper classes –

> *many years of experience and observation have proved to me, that this disorder has not its origin in good cheer, but in excess of other kinds ...A copious and sustained exercise is the surest preventive ... that bodily activity which, occasioning fatigue, would enable them to enjoy the sweets of repose ... nature affords a simple remedy against the abuse of good cheer – Abstinence.*

Indeed, Ude was accused by his rivals of starving the nation to death when he introduced the light Sandwich

Supper to the fashionable Regency routs and soirees.
Byron would have approved –

*I am going to R—'s tonight – to one of those suppers
which* ought *to be dinners.*

LETTER TO THOMAS MOORE, JUNE 14th, 1814.

But the recipes are certainly elaborate and complicated –

*The Author could recommend a skilfully dressed
dish as in all respects more salubrious than
simple fare.*

and Byron chooses a dozen, though of course there would
have been many more dishes for each of the two courses
of a grand Regency dinner. They are all more or less
comprehensible to the modern cook – cock's combs and
truffles being the only ingredients likely to pose problems
for any enthusiastic amateur wishing to reproduce this
dinner in all its glory.

For the rest is required only, in the words of M. Ude –

*a most diligent and studious application, no small
share of intellect, and the strictest sobriety
and punctuality.*

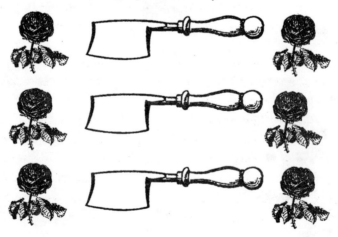

THE EDITOR'S POSTSCRIPT:
LORD BYRON'S EATING HABITS

LORD BYRON'S eating habits have long been a subject of discussion and are well documented, by himself and by his family and friends. In looking closely at them, at his social habits in general and at the relationship between these and his sexual behaviour, a remarkably clear picture has emerged of the condition named by Sir William Gull 49 years after the poet's death – *anorexia nervosa*. The outstanding feature of this condition is "the relentless pursuit of excessive thinness". The word anorexia means loss of appetite (via new Latin from Greek, from *an- + orexis,* appetite) but this is misleading as a true anorexic is preoccupied with food to the point of obsession.

The illness generally affects healthy pubescent or adolescent subjects (mostly female, and from privileged backgrounds) and it is frequently triggered off by an exaggerated approach to dieting because the person feels, or is, fat. Often there is an older member of the family who is overweight, and not infrequently the young person is faced with a new or difficult situation or is deprived of familiar supports. It is generally believed that anorexia is related to deep-seated feelings of insecurity and anxiety. Self-denial and discipline are of supreme importance to the anorexic but there is also a degree of exhibitionism. In order to demonstrate control over biological urges, and to reach the ultimate goal of extreme thinness, anorexics will starve for long periods, train themselves to enjoy the sensation of hunger and indulge in exhausting exercise (often solitary) in an effort to burn off calories. They take great pride in the weight loss (which can be dramatic) and in their emaciated appearance. If the urge to satisfy their hunger becomes uncontrollable, they can eat prodigious quantities only to be overcome with feelings of disgust and guilt which can only be relieved by self-induced vomiting, the use of strong purgatives and an even more stringent programme of fasting.

When Byron went up to Trinity College, Cambridge in 1805 at the age of 17½, he was *miserable and untoward to a degree",– "a fat bashful boy"* with a club foot. He was *"wretched at leaving Harrow"* where he had at last settled down, and unhappy at going to Cambridge instead of Oxford where there were no available rooms. Mary Chaworth, the girl he had loved since 1803, had recently married, and relations with his mother were steadily declining.

> *I have never been so scurrilously and violently abused by any person,* [he wrote to his half-sister Augusta] *as by that woman ... whom I am sorry I cannot love or admire.*

However, thrown into the deep end at Trinity he managed to conquer his natural diffidence enough to participate in the life of debauchery expected of a young nobleman there – though more out of a sense of duty, than from natural inclination.

> *I took my gradations in the vices with great promptitude, but they were not to my taste ... I could not share in the common place libertinism of the*

place and time without disgust.

He became more and more melancholy, and grew steadily fatter, so that by autumn, 1806 he was 14 stone 6lb – an enormous weight for a young man of only 5ft 8 ½ in. That he suffered on account of his fatness as well as his lameness is probable, and when he adopted his "System" of weight reduction early in 1807 it was *"on account of a Bet with an acquaintance"* – more than a hint here of the teasing that can set off a potential anorexic – though no doubt his mother's obesity was also a significant factor. The "System" was fanatical enough.

> *I have taken every means to accomplish the end, by violent exercise, & Fasting, as I found myself too plump. – I shall continue my Exertions, having no other amusements, I wear seven Waistcoats, & a great Coat, run & play Cricket in this Dress, till quite exhausted by excessive perspiration, use the hot Bath daily, eat only a quarter of* [a] *pound* [of] *Butchers meat in 24 hours, no Suppers, or Breakfast, only one meal a Day, drink no malt liquor,* [only] *little Wine, & take physic occasionally ...*

It certainly proved effective, and by April 16, 1807, he had lost 23lb, by April 19 a further 4lb bringing his weight down to 12 stone 7lb and by August 20 he was unrecognisable.

> *I am grown ... so much thinner from illness and violent exercise, that many who have lived with me in habits of intimacy, even old Schoolfellows, found great difficulty in acknowledging me to be the same person.*

And the regime continued with various modifications: in

July 1811 he was 9 stone 11 ½ lb by which time he was a *"Leguminous-eating Ascetic"* and anxious to remain so, as can be seen by his letter to his mother that summer, announcing his imminent arrival at Newstead.

> *I must only inform you that for a long time I have been restricted to an entire vegetable diet, neither fish nor flesh coming within my regimin, so I expect a powerful stock of potatoes, greens, and biscuits, I drink no wine … I have only to beg you will not forget my diet, which it is very necessary for me to observe.*

That thinness was important to him all his life is plain from the frequency with which the subject crops up in "the Letters". That it was also a matter of pride to appear thin to the point of unrecognisability is clear from reports from friends such as Lady Blessington.

> *Nothing gratifies him so much as being told that he grows thin … [and] 'Did you ever see any person so thin as I am who was not ill,' he frequently asks.*

But he also had a true gourmet's appreciation of all kinds of food and of The Art of Cookery, and he hated *"the perpetual lamentations after beef and beer"* of the Englishman abroad – *"the stupid bigotted contempt for everything foreign."* This apparent paradox – a lively interest in food coupled with the desire for self-starvation – is characteristic of the anorexic, as is the wish to feed others. Byron enjoyed entertaining, whether it was the tenants at Newstead, or his college friends, or the Shelley circle at Pisa where he held lavish weekly dinners (there is one surviving menu) even while on spartan rations himself.

His friends were indulgent of his eccentricities but were not always able to cope. Samuel Rogers told a story (much quoted) of how Byron dined with him for the first time. He refused soup, fish, meat, wine, asked for biscuits and soda water, and when these were not to be had, dined on potatoes mashed up with vinegar. (probably the idea of potatoes as a slimming food came from the *Treatise on Corpulence* which he had lately purchased.) Later that evening it was reported that he went to a club in St James Street and consumed a large meat supper – a tale which Doris Langley Moore considers improbable since Thomas Moore talks of the potato meal being a "hearty" one. But in fact, gorging and particularly secret indulgence is characteristic of the anorexic, and such a diagnosis in Byron's case would go a long way towards explaining his bizarre and antisocial behaviour with his wife and parents-in-law.

"Lord Byron was in the habit of dining alone." Hobhouse too, had noted in his journal, *"He does not dine with his wife"* – and Medwin was told by Byron: *"I have prejudices about women: I do not like to see them eat."*

"For 4 or 5 months before my confinement," wrote Lady Byron, *"he objected unkindly to dine with me ... and once when his dinner was accidentally served at the same table as mine, he desired his dish, to be taken into another room (in my presence, and the servants attending) with an expression of rage."* Byron himself, had earlier written to Lady Melbourne about his latest love in Italy,

> *I only wish she did not swallow so much supper ... women should never be seen eating or drinking, unless it be lobster sallad and Champagne.*

THE EDITOR'S POSTSCRIPT:

But I would suggest that Byron's horror was not so much at seeing women eat as at being seen by them in the act of eating. Even Teresa Guiccioli with whome he was on more intimate terms than with any other woman, was rarely allowed to dine with him. The anorexic's self-disgust crops up frequently in the letters, and with it, the suggestion of attendant physical discomforts. As Augusta wrote to Annabella.

> *I am quite convinc'd that if he would condescend to eat and drink and sleep like other people he would feel ye good effects – but you know his way is to fast till he is famished and then devour more than his stomach in that weak state can bear.*

"When I do *dine*," Byron writes, "*I gorge like an Arab or a Boa snake.*" And so a pattern emerges, of gorging – fasting – gorging – remorse and purging, and physical discomfort. "*I have dined regularly today, for the first time since Sunday last,*" he wrote in 1813.

> *... this being Sabbath, too. All the rest, tea and dry biscuits – six per diem. I wish to God I had not dined now! – It kills me with heaviness, stupor, and horrible dreams ... I wish I were in the country, to take exercise, – instead of being obliged to cool by abstinence ... I should not so much mind a little accession of flesh – my bones can well bear it. But the worst is, the devil always came with it, till I starve him out, – and I will not be the slave of any appetite.*

There is no doubt of the sexual implication here, and it is interesting to note that Byron was at his fattest while indulging in his greatest sexual excesses – in 1806, while at Cambridge and much later while expatriate in Venice in 1818, some two years after the separation from Annabella. He had a constant fear of being dominated by animal appetites and *"the vulture passions"* and this was one of the reasons why he tried to resist meat all his life. He believed that animal food *"engenders the appetite of the animal fed upon"* and that it was only by abstinence that he felt he had the power of exercising his mind.

This idea of mind over matter is frequently demonstrated by the anorexic in enduring great physical hardship and in driving the body to extremes, even when it is weak as a result of chronic malnutrition. Byron was, from his schooldays, a strong swimmer, and very proud of the fact. Indeed, when Lady Blessington accuses him of vanity, she produces against him *"his boasts of swimming"*.

As early as 1809 he had impressed Hobhouse *"by swimming from old Lisbon to Belem Castle, and having to contend with a tide, and counter current ... but little less than two hours in crossing the river."* And the following year he was writing to his friends of his romantic swim of the Hellespont – in imitation of Leander.

> *I shall content myself with stating my only remark-*
> *able personal achievement, namely swimming from*
> *Sestos to Abydos ... as it made an ancient immortal,*
> *I see no reason why a modern may not be permitted*
> *to boast of it ...*

Byron made himself ill more than once (notably on the occasion of Shelley's cremation at Viareggio) by swimming long distances in inclement weather, but it took Pietro

Gamba's perception to see that this kind of physical endurance was psychologically necessary to him, as he wrote to his sister Teresa.

> *To tell you the truth, I have never seen him in better health than in the midst of the greatest hardships. Riding eight hours a day under a broiling sun in August, he was perfectly well. Sleeping for eight nights without undressing on board a miserable brig in the rawest December, and bathing in the sea in that season (all folly) he could not have been better.*

But two months later the poet was dead. He appeared to have been intensifying the regime towards the end of his life – the refusals of dinner invitations had become more explicit –

> *I dare not venture to dine with you, tomorrow nor indeed any day this week*

to Lord Blessington in April 1823, and a month later to the same man –

> *I hope you will not take my not dining with you again after so many dinners, ill; but the truth is that your banquets are too luxurious for my habits.*

He did, however, sometimes dine with the Blessingtons and Lady Blessington told of one occasion when he partook of two helpings of plum pudding *à l'Anglaise*.

> *He hoped he should not shock us by eating so much:*
> *'But,' added he, 'the truth is, that for several months I have been following a most abstemious régime ... and now that I see a good dinner, I cannot resist temptation, though tomorrow I shall suffer for my*

gourmandise ...

There had been a plum pudding too, two years before in Ravenna.

Dined versus six o' clock. Forgot that there was a plum-pudding. (I have added, lately, eating to my 'family of vices') and had dined before I knew it.

But these were exceptions and most of the time *"he was eating very little"* although very thin indeed. Until the end of his life he remained obsessed with his appearance and felt compelled to write to all his friends to tell them just how thin he was – to Douglas Kinnaird – December 1, 1822 –

I have subsided into my former more meagre outline ...

and to Hoppner only a month later –

I am thin as a Skeleton – thinner than you saw me at my first arrival in Venice – and thinner than yourself – there's a climax!

Two months later he was writing to Thomas Moore.

I am thin, – perhaps thinner than you saw me, when I was nearly transparent, in 1812, – and am obliged to be moderate of my mouth.

And although so thin and generally abstemious, he continued to consume quantities of vinegar (another characteristic anorexic taste), to use strong purgative pills, and to dose himself with Epsom salts and the like.

The thing that gives me the highest spirits (it seems absurd, but true) is a dose of salts – I mean in the afternoon, after their effect.

And Trewlaney reports of Byron saying *"I am always better after vomiting."* It had become quite impossible for him to change his way of life, to do without the salts and fasting

*FROM A DRAWING OF BYRON
BY COUNT ALFRED D'ORSAY, 1823*

and the purgatives, and the over-all picture is one of great sadness – *"If you had my life, indeed,"* he wrote to Moore in 1881,

> *... changing climates and connections – thinning yourself with fasting and purgatives – besides the wear and tear of the vulture passions, and a very bad temper besides, you might talk in this way – but you! I know no man who looks so well for his years, or who deserves to look better and to be better, in all respects ... So don't talk of decay, but put in for eighty, as you well may.*

Byron died at thirty six.

Putting the evidence together, his habits seem to match the major conditions for, and symptoms of, *anorexia nervosa* point for point. His background was privileged, he had an obese parent whom he despised, he was himself fat and acutely self-conscious. As for the symptoms, they read like a case history: alternate fasting and binging, excessive exercise (particularly swimming), regular purging of the system (even a suggestion of self-induced vomiting), a desire not to be seen eating, an association between gastric and sexual appetite, a taste for vinegar and highly spiced foods, and a constant desire to appear thin to the point of emaciation.

It has often been thought that Byron's life was one of a constant gratification of the appetites, but it would seem that in fact he suffered from a horrifying alternation of repletion and revulsion which can have brought him little satisfaction. The sense of disillusionment that this must have engendered is found throughout his work and many of the peculiar anxieties of the anorexic may well be found to underly both the choice of subject-matter and its treatment, particularly in *Don Juan*, a poem which he never finished and in which the asssociation of sexual and gastric preoccupations is particularly strong. There is no doubt that Byron's life was highly spiced, but it would seem this was more a neurotic necessity to him than a source of pleasure.

If I was born, as the nurses say, with a 'silver spoon in my mouth,' it has stuck in my throat, and spoiled my palate, so that nothing put into it is swallowed with much relish, – unless it be cayenne.

BIBLIOGRAPHY
COOKERY BOOKS

GLASSE, Mrs Hannah:
  The Art of Cookery made Plain and Easy, 1747
MOXON, Elizabeth:
  English Housewifery Exemplified, 1749
RAFFALD, Mrs Elizabeth:
  The Experienced English Housekeeper, 1769
MASON, Mrs Charlotte: *The Ladies' Assistant
          and Complete System of Cookery, 1773*
NUTT, Frederick: *The Complete Confectioner, 1789*
MILLINGTON, Charles:
  The Housekeeper's Domestic Library, 1805
RUNDELL, Mrs: *A New System of DomesticCookery,
    1806   The New Family Receipt Book, 1815*
UDE, Louis Eustache: *The French Cook, 1813*
ibid.   *The French Cook, 1827*
KITCHINER, William, M.D. *The Cook's Oracle, 1817*
DODS, Mrs. Margaret   *The Cook and Housewife's
    Manual, 1826,   Hints for the Table, 1860*

BYRON

ORIGO, Iris   *The Last Attachment, 1949*
MARCHAND, Leslie A.   *Byron, a Biography, 1958*
ELWIN, Malcolm   *Lord Byron's Wife, 1962*
LOVELL, Ernest J.   *Lady Blessington's
          Conversations of Lord Byron, 1969*
MOORE, Doris L.   *Accounts Rendered, 1974*
MARCHAND, Leslie A.
    Byron's Letters and Journals, 1973–81